Debt Free and Set for Life

Debt Free and Set for Life

✦

Become Wealthy and Live Your Dreams

Les J. Tripp, MBA

iUniverse, Inc.
New York Lincoln Shanghai

Debt Free and Set for Life
Become Wealthy and Live Your Dreams

iUniverse books may be ordered through booksellers or by contacting:

iUniverse
2021 Pine Lake Road, Suite 100
Lincoln, NE 68512
www.iuniverse.com
1-800-Authors (1-800-288-4677)

Because of the dynamic nature of the Internet, any Web addresses or links contained in this book may have changed since publication and may no longer be valid.

The information, ideas, and suggestions in this book are not intended to render professional advice. Before following any suggestions contained in this book, you should consult your personal accountant or other financial advisor. Neither the author nor the publisher shall be liable or responsible for any loss or damage allegedly arising as a consequence of your use or application of any information or suggestions in this book.

ISBN: 978-0-595-44741-1 (pbk)
ISBN: 978-0-595-68962-0 (cloth)
ISBN: 978-0-595-89062-0 (ebk)

Printed in the United States of America

This book is for anyone who wants to become wealthy and live his or her dreams.

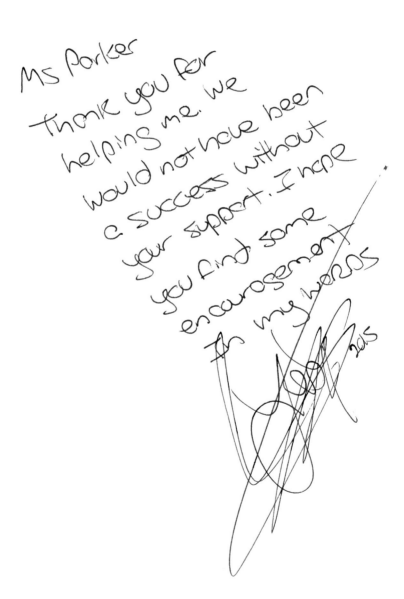

Ms Porker

Thank you for helping me. We would not have been a success without your support. I hope you find some encouragement in my words

2015

To each person who tries to lessen the burdens of life on another.

In memory of
Grandmother Teresa Mclean, C. H. Tripp, Glenn Richardson and Judge Michael W. Lee

Contents

Acknowledgments

Special thanks to:

My Mother, Teresa Tripp
Tara Kearney (Chief Motivator)
Nick Waddy
Gary DeShields
Greggory Jones
Joe Martin—Mentor, real estate advisor, personal friend
Craig and Sharon Gendler—friends and family

Dr. Gibson and Dr. Jackson
Dr. Mahesh Mittal—encouragement and academic inspiration
Dr. Kam Ghaffarian—encouragement to finish my MBA

Special thanks to Guy Samon, Todd Lomax, and Larry Aaronson for always providing intelligent and trustworthy counsel.

Preface

Thank you for purchasing *Debt Free & Set for Life.*

The road to financial success is not the path of least resistance. It is not the status quo for most people in the United States, nor what they expect. Consider who sets those expectations. The culture that we live in is defined by America's wealthy elite and has plenty of ways to dampen creativity, ambition, and the wish to succeed. To succeed in America, you must become entrepreneurial in your thinking. You must decide to become wealthy.

It is easy to cite the high number of families turned down for mortgage loans, management positions, and business opportunities. And it is easy to cite the number of people who live in quiet desperation while the wealth of America flourishes. These statistics prove only that the American dream appears beyond the grasp of many people in America.

Gainful employment is often a beginning, but it is not the long-term answer that people should seek. Gainful employment is usually sustained by the ability to solve problems for an employer. Successful entrepreneurs and independent thinking people like you will develop the ability to solve financial problems for themselves and potential clients. Each of us working for someone else must realize that despite the job we are really self-employed. The privilege of self-employment means being responsible for your own education, career advancement, wealth, and retirement.

Foolish is the person who does not continue their education just because their employer does not offer tuition reimbursement or will not provide funds to help them move up along their chosen career path. Yet people are foolish and take offense at the lack of services provided by their company without considering whether the company has the economic base to offer those services. Successful entrepreneurs take responsibility for their own success. When people realize that their position in life, both economic and social, is a direct function of their mindset, attitude, and actions, the road to freedom and success begins.

Circumstances that interfere with becoming debt free and set for life are to be expected. These circumstances become problematic only if not anticipated. Success requires vision, belief and hard work.

There is no king who has not had a slave among his ancestors, and no slave who has not had a king among his ancestors.

—Helen Keller, *The Story of My Life*

Obstacles exist to be overcome. If a society descended from kings and queens, scientists and philosophers, becomes enslaved, it has only to learn from the history of success in order to rise again, free and higher than before.

You can become a successful entrepreneur only by learning from your own successes and the successes and failures of those who have traveled before you.

PART I
Become Debt Free

1

Create Your Own Destiny

You must strengthen your ability to take positive action in your life. This simple statement begins the power of making decisions. The act of being decisive or complacent separates the dreamers from the capitalists in America. Decisions are largely responsible for separating the happy and elated from the mildly depressed. Instead of setting your sights on your desires, set them around your decisions. Proceed in your life as though you could not fail.

To be truly successful in any endeavor you must strengthen your ability to take positive action in your life. This simple statement begins the power of making decisions. Decisiveness separates the dreamers from the capitalists in America. Decisions are largely responsible for separating the happy and successful from the many people who live in quiet desperation.Instead of defining accomplishment in terms of your hopes and dreams, define them in terms of your decisions. Proceed in life as though you could not fail.

Wealth Tip

Do not let your life be based on your existing problems; base your life on your future potential instead. This decision is yours to make and can be as simple as changing the way you think. Many people do not achieve their goals in life because of what they choose to think about. Many people focus on what they lack instead of what they want.

Take sound and meaningful actions toward your goals. This idea sounds obvious. The best ideas, practices, and methodologies usually are the simplest. You must decide that you have endured the stressful pains of financial bondage long enough. You must decide to become free. Define your freedom in writing. Define your freedom as ending the bondage of your debts. Define your freedom in terms of time for unrestricted travel or family time with your loved ones. Contrary to what you see on television, freedom is not a Porsche or a BMW convertible but rather the time to enjoy a vehicle without the restrictions imposed by work or bill payments.

Great things in life may appear serendipitously, but more often they come because we have made a decision to seek great things. Higher goals are defined by the individual and often include spiritual, religious, and personal goals.

Freedom from debt obligations and entrapping employment starts with a decision. Decide today that you are no longer going to live in debt.

Use the philosophy of Debtors Anonymous, which teaches that freedom from debt begins by not creating any new debt today. Life is not a long and gloomy look at the past or a fearful look into the future. A successful life begins with controlling the present and the moments that you have the most control over. The past is gone; the future is an illusion to be planned and hoped for. The only chance you have to create lasting meaning in your life is the present moment. A successful life will be a stream of successful moments organized into daily goals, weekly goals, and higher goals reached through consistent effort. Decide that you are not going to create any new debt today. Decide that you are going to become wealthy in America.

Decide to keep a log of your spending. Track how long you can go without charging anything. Create no new debts, starting with today. Set a goal to create no new debts, one day at a time. Each day as you arise, decide to create no new debt and to enjoy the day. Decide to become wealthy and financially independent at some point in your life. Brian Tracy, in his influential work, *Getting Rich in America*, states that most people living in America do not become rich because they have never decided to become rich.

Create the belief, and the plan and the actions will soon follow. Decide upon your goal and then learn how to take the necessary steps to meet your goal. Changing any process or action will involve reading and learning, and perhaps taking a class on savings and investments; decide that this is what you are going to do. You must understand that everything that you have learned to get to the present stage in your life will not necessarily get you to the next stage. Everything you learned in grade school up to the third grade helped you but did not guarantee that you would complete the fourth grade. Life is the same. Many people will work on a job for twenty years, literally repeating the same work with the same level of effort over and over again. Decide to be different. Write down what you have done that has been successful and what has been less than successful. Strive not to repeat the problems you had the year before. If you have ever bounced a check, try to never bounce a check again. If you have spent your last dollar, commit yourself to always having a ten or a hundred in a separate place in your wallet, so that you will never again spend your last dollar.

Realize that your old financial self will not carry you forward into the future. Decide to start over today and move with confidence in a positive direction.

As I mentioned earlier, Brian Tracy thinks that most people in America do not become rich because they never decide to become rich. It has never occurred to them that with all of the resources, education, and opportunities in this country, most working people in America could retire wealthy simply by executing a proper plan.

Dreams are essential, but decisions lay the foundations for success. Decide today that you are not going to settle for anything less than your dreams. *Getting Rich in America* by Brian Tracy was certainly a book that changed my life.

Wealth Tip

Many families in America will earn more than $1 million in their lifetime but will not become wealthy because they never decided to become wealthy. If they have not made the decision to become wealthy, they will not do the research, study, or make the proper investments, nor will they plan to save and invest some of the money that they make. All this, despite the fact that the average family with a income of $40,000 a year and a career lasting forty years will earn $1.6 million.

There are at least three ways to make money.

The most common way is to exchange your time for money by the hour. Although this is the most common way, it is also the hardest way to become rich. Your time and your life are quite finite. By the time you have exchanged enough of your time for enough money to feel rich, much of your life has passed. And while your life was passing you may have ignored many wonderful things simply because you could not afford to spend less of your time making money or spending the money that you may have accumulated. This method of financial achievement is a treadmill. You start working for an hourly wage when you are young. If you progress through school, moving from job to job as everyone does, you will begin to earn more money per hour. It seems easy to conclude that success will come from earning a higher and higher wage. The reality is that this form of income is active income. True wealth, however, usually comes from passive income. As I have said before, with active income you work for your money, with passive income your money and your investments work for you. This is why many doctors and lawyers, who have a high hourly wage in our society, learn about investments in order to multiply their money.

The second method is investing in market economies and letting your investments compound in interest and principal. If you are very good, this can be one of the best ways to become wealthy, provided you have the knowledge base and the capital required. An example of this would be investing in the stock, options, or commodities market.

The third method is getting other people to exchange their labor or skills for you and creating multiple streams of income. This method is lucrative and has produced many more millionaires than the other two methods combined. Multi-level marketing, distributor-based businesses, temporary services, and franchising a business are examples of this method.

The conundrum here is that these methods only work to your benefit if you know about them!

As Thoreau so profoundly stated, "the mass of men lead lives of quiet desperation." Often the resentment, frustration, and even hatred you see in other people are a reflection of some pain or lack of accomplishment in their own lives.

2

Everyone Has a Story

My story starts in Liverpool, England. My mother married an American, an enlisted man in the air force, and we moved to America when I was a child. When I was in sixth grade in the public school system, I started to see some of the inequities that are prevalent in society, although at that age I certainly did not understand their significance. I had friends of different ethnic and cultural backgrounds, but even as a child I noticed some differences. Little did I know that such differences could have long-lasting social and financial ramifications? My school friends usually lived in houses. My neighborhood friends and my family always lived in apartments. The parents of my schoolmates drove nice cars, often new but never very flashy. But my friends and family looked in awe at people in the community who bought large flashy automobiles, no matter what the cost. Only later did I learn that most of these cars were financed; many had little actual value other than what the owner owed the bank that financed the car. The apartments we lived in were always well decorated. My mother and father would put up expensive wallpaper, buy different types of paint, and really apply their creativity and talent in making our apartment a home. My mother was clearly an interior design expert waiting to find a canvas.

In retrospect I can now see the impact of those times. As I struggled to find the money to start my first business, many of my school friends from other communities were given their first starter home by their parents, as their parents moved onward and upward. A home that has been in the family for many years generally has some equity, which can be borrowed against or used as collateral for educational or business loans.

My path to success would not be easy, but it would be attainable. I would soon discover, as I applied for credit for my business enterprises, how useful a fixed asset and a negotiated mortgage could be. I had neither, but what I really lacked was the education and experience that my family had not been able to pass down. Each dollar we spent in those beautiful apartments went toward making someone else rich. Year after year my parents would pay rent without as much as a single tax deduction. My family, like the families of my peer group, would spend thousands of dollars making homes of apartments while driving around in some new expensive automobile. People, who have not yet gained financial independence, want the same goals and ideals for their family as everyone else who embraces the American Dream. With my family, our greatest asset was the net worth, often negative, of some car. Naturally, like most young men, I fell in love with cars. They symbolized the freedom and excitement that would become part of my burning desire to get ahead in life. My first car brought me the freedom to travel. I traveled and explored some of the hotels and office buildings in the impressive city of Baltimore.

One day in Baltimore, celebrating my mother's birthday, I treated her to lunch at the Grand Hyatt. Sitting in that building, looking out over the harbor, I dreamed a dream that I have to this day. My dream was to own such a hotel. I came to the realization that there was a level of life that I was not seeing because of the limited surroundings of my social and work circles. I dedicated myself to the study of real estate and acquisition in the hopes that this would give me the freedom in life I had always wanted. I would spend the next twenty years finishing college and working at some great jobs; meanwhile, I started acquiring residential properties and studying every method of business and real estate acquisition that I could find. I became an independent computer consultant, started an import/export management company, and provided financial backing for two video stores, all the while investing in real estate. I read every no-money-down, tax-lien scheme and plan that came along. I found that the people who put on the no-money-down seminars had all written books that could be obtained for much less than the cost of attending the actual seminar. Since I was putting myself through school, I had little discretionary income, and yet I always believed it was a good idea to see if I could envision something greater. While the values of my business enterprises rose and fell with the stock market, one thing remained constant, my real estate investments. I purchased wisely, below market value, timed the acquisition for good rental months, and always wrote the advertisement long before I bought the property.

After my thirty-first birthday I was a little dejected about not having really made a mark for myself in any of my business ventures. I was working in Lotus 1-2-3, studying my spreadsheets, when I came to an interesting discovery. My portfolio of real estate alone had grown to over $1 million dollars worth of property, which produced positive cash flow. The income from my real-estate investments exceeded the income from some of the nice jobs I had had after graduating from college. The best part about the real estate income was that it was passive income. My properties did not care if I worked that day or not.

Wealth tip

Passive Income is defined as earnings an individual derives from a rental property, limited partnership, or other enterprise in which he or she is not actively involved. According to Dictionary.com

---

As with anything else that I get involved in, I began to study real estate with passion and vigor. My stepfather told me as a child that if I studied anything with passion and determination, I would one day become rich. Studying real estate led me to see the big picture of how debt, credit, and values are woven together in America. Although most people earn a small fortune during their lifetime, the interaction of debt, credit, and values often leaves them consumed by debt; they fall victim to credit traps and never reach their full potential.

Opportunity in America is as plentiful as money, and like money, opportunity comes with no instructions. This book attempts to provide some of the instructions observations, techniques, and experiences that have benefited me along the path, a path that I continue to follow. My hope is that more people learn to profit from the incredible wealth in America, wealth that is available to most, often hidden in the form of books!

3

Get Out of Debt

o o o o o o o o o o o o o o o o o o o o o o o o o o o o o o o o o o o

For there is nothing either good or bad, but thinking makes it so.

—**Shakespeare,** *Hamlet*

There is life after debt. There is also life during debt. Though often it is just the constrained life of bill collectors and bad credit or a life filled with emptiness and the feelings of helplessness that come from not having any credit, it can become a good life, a productive and rewarding life. We must never forget that we are not living to pay our bills but are living to enjoy life. Creditors give us bills, but life was given to us by our creator. Realizing that you must not lose your perspective just because you are in debt is a major step toward recovering from debt and reestablishing your self-esteem.

War Stories

Interviewing numerous people for the book, I found variations of several stories of why or how people get into debt. Some people became overextended without realizing how their actions could and would produce long-term debt. It is difficult, after all, to see how a ten-dollar credit purchase could lead to excessive long-term debt. Others were success-oriented wealth-builders who had dreams and plans to conquer the financial community. Credit was seen as a means to the end: wealth and prosperity. Most people simply never considered the implications of their spending habits. Fifty-dollar ties and two-hundred-dollar dresses were just part of the ritual of life, each item comfortably purchased on one of their credit cards. Many people that I talked to had gotten into debt with their first car, developed poor payment habits, and became years older and yet no wiser, despite their misery. Many of these people are still driving that first car that led them down the road to debt. Surprisingly, the car may be a moderately old BMW or

10

Mercedes-Benz. I am an automobile enthusiast and car club member, but even I do not see the sense in purchasing such a status symbol before the appropriate time, particularly if it then becomes a hindrance to your success. In 2006, according to the Maryland Coalition for Financial Literacy, credit-card payments were the primary reason young people dropped out of college. This is a tragedy. College should mark the beginning of the best investment a person will ever make in their life, not the beginning of repaying the worst debt in their life.

Credit Card Debt

The number one reason college students dropped out of school in 2006, according to the Maryland Coalition for Financial Literacy.

4

The Benefits of Being Debt Free

The secret of happiness is freedom, and the secret of freedom, courage.

—Thucydides

Many words and books have been written about debt, credit, and management of debt. Educational debt and real estate debt are good types of debt. But commercial debt is bad; this includes credit cards, department store charges, and lines of credit. Being completely free of debt is great, but it is unlikely that you will be free of debt unless you are independently wealthy or have a tremendous source of passive income. Having income-producing debt is the reality of most wealthy people in America. Understand clearly that this means they have purchased income-generating assets on credit. According to U.S. census data, the two things most wealthy people have in common are the ownership of real estate and an advanced education. Notice that I did not say an excessive number of high-interest credit cards.

Many people have become so indoctrinated into living in debt that they cannot imagine life without credit cards, debt, and monthly payments. This is sad. Children are not born in debt. No one should spend the rest of their life chained to a job in order to pay off credit cards, their home mortgage, and their few possessions, yet this is exactly what happens in our society. Because of recent changes in bankruptcy laws and credit-servicing laws, most people in our modern American society will remain in debt forever. They will live in debt, and they will die in debt. The government has already determined that most people cannot live independently when they retire with social security benefits unless they have help from their family or continue to work. Many seniors cannot support themselves without working full or part time to make ends meet. This is sad. No one deserves to work in the richest country on earth, in the richest country of all time, just to die in debt, working their last days still trying to make monthly payments. Unfortunately, this is what we let happen by not paying attention to what our banking and credit industry has been doing for the past hundred years.

Imagine not having to pay interest or borrow money to pay for life's two biggest necessities, transportation and housing. Most people cannot. Yet there are many people in this country who live the life that you may have only dreamed of. You can become one of these people by using the system to your benefit, as opposed to being a victim of the system. You can eliminate all of the commercial debt in your life, debt that drains the life out of you for most of your life. Turning the pain of commercial debt into the leverage of real-estate debt can lead to wealth. More importantly, consider what debt is doing to your family. What are you teaching your children about debt, credit-card payments, and life? Statistics show that your children will probably not be as financially successful as you. Do you want them to live a life of trampled dreams, struggling to pay off Visa and MasterCard?

Most people spend their lives monitoring their credit scores, watching their bank accounts to see when their direct deposit arrives, and planning their next credit purchase. What if you did not have to live that lifestyle? What if you did not have credit scores to watch because you have cash? What if you could leave your children your home, paid off and mortgage free? What if you had inherited a home from your parents? How would your life be different today?

A life worth living is a life dedicated to your beliefs, your family, and your personal freedoms.

We have come to accept being in debt and burdened by jobs we hate as the standard form of life. None of us were born to support credit-card companies. Each of us was born with our own spark of life and for life. You owe it to yourself not to let your spark burn any less brightly because of the burden put on you by excessive debt, excessive interest, and excessive fees. Your life was created to enjoy, not being lost in the despair of bad debts.

Caged birds accept each other but flight is what they long for.

—Tennessee Williams

5

Social Standing

Social standing and how it can hold you back!

Don't try to be better than your contemporaries or your predecessors try to be better than yourself

—William Faulkner

Social standing can be one of the greatest impediments to your success. Since the beginning of time, people have tended to seek a higher or more acceptable social status. This occurs naturally within most social groups. Part of human development is the need to be accepted, to fit in, and then to be emulated by others in your condition.

Society has strongly criticizes the house slaves without seeing any of the parallels to modern society. As a community we spend millions of dollars trying to present a better image than our peers. The expression "keeping up with the Jones's" is even more relevant today, for with the gains in Internet communications, we can now see what the Jones's everywhere are buying. Keeping up with the Jones's is not necessarily problematic. Going into debt is problematic. The problems occur when you come to believe that elevated social status is based on those largely material purchases. Remember that Emerson defined freedom in terms of the number of things you can live without.

The average consumer often fall into the trap of trying to maintain the appearance of the elevated social status that a well-paying job can bring, while ignoring the concept of real wealth where investments and money work for you. This consumer will regularly drive an expensive, new foreign car, either leased or purchased by loan, with monthly payments that seriously cut into his cash flow. Buying new suits on credit, charging everything right down to his socks, this person looks good but maintains a level of debt that keeps him in a financial prison.

This consumer may never accumulate enough money to start a business and will often not produce enough to finish funding their education.

This consumer may try to empower themselves by looking down on others who are not as fortunate (and probably not as much in debt). Shunning people who do not or cannot measure up to some false set of standards is a part of the image taught by our media savvy culture, often by characters on television.

Wealth Tip

In life you will miss every shot you do not take.

You must be careful not to make the error of seeing people in grandiose or unrealistic terms. Many people who are millionaires are actually much richer than they appear, while it is an interesting irony that people who are not millionaires generally appear richer than they really are. Thomas Stanley and William Danko discuss this phenomenon in their landmark book, *The Millionaire Next Door*.

With each purchase, ask yourself the question: is this expense contributing to my wealth, or taking away from it?

> *Too many people spend money they haven't earned to buy things they don't want to impress people they don't like.*

—Unknown

6

Personal Power

o o o o o o o o o o o o o o o o o o o o o o o o o o o o o o o o o o o

*If you are bored with life ... you don't get up every morning with a
burning desire to do things ... you don't have enough goals.*

—*Lou Holtz*

One personal story began during my early college days. A friend worked at a local
shoe store. To make ends meet, he worked long and hard. Every day he would see
customers enter and purchase extremely expensive athletic items. Most of the
purchases were made with credit cards. Surprisingly, many of the purchases were
gifts.

It seems that it is easier to go into debt buying for other people than buying
for ourselves. A sense of public good and personal accommodation of others is
thought to be higher than accommodating one's own needs, which may be perceived as selfish. The power brought by purchasing was what most impressed my
friend.

Those who work in retail or in an office from nine to five easily see why any form
of liberal spending can yield a sense of power. How many times have you been
feeling down or depressed and gotten a lift simply by purchasing something? People often lead lives of quiet desperation, reveling in the hope that things will get
better. Each time they create a little more debt, they take themselves further away
form the goal of financial success. Having the ability to buy gifts for friends and
family or to charge a vacation or weekend trip and get approved with just one
phone call can instill a sense of power. People become victims of maintaining the
appearance of wealth, as will be discussed in a later chapter. Maintaining this illusion often occurs at the expense of real wealth.

In my colleges days I saw that many people regarded the very appearance of having money and power as excellent in itself. At the center of this overwhelming fantasy was the realization that anyone could have obtained this power. Surely one credit card would lead to another and then another. In college, I, would build a strong credit foundation and seek gold credit cards. There were commercials on television and seminars advertising that you could become a credit card millionaire. But the day my first credit card came in the mail was my beginning and almost became my end. It would take years of study, learning from mentors and strangers, before I would overcome my early credit card additions.

That first credit card started a process that would change my life forever. I would never again be the same person. I gladly accepted my first credit card. I anticipated the power it would bring. I applied for and received another, then another. Seven credit cards in all and one was even a gold card. I was set, or so I thought.

When I could not afford to work and finish college, I said "No problem!" and then paid my rent with a cash advance on Visa Gold. When I needed to buy Christmas or birthday gifts, again, "No problem!" and I charged them. I graduated and, with a technical degree in hand, set out to find stable employment in the computer field. Of course, this process required several months of looking, since I proceeded at a rather comfortable pace. My pace was comfortable because I had plenty of cash-advance money at 21 percent interest to carry me through! Today those interest rates are escalating; the highest that I have seen is 39 percent.

If you have built castles in the air, your work need not be lost; that is where they should be. Now put the foundations under them.

—Henry David Thoreau

My situation was worsening, yet I had too much purchasing power to see it. I foolishly compared myself to so many of my friends who were in debt because they had purchased new cars. My excuse was that since I had no monthly payment for a new car I could afford to maintain my pyramiding debt. Even as I obtained cash advances to buy the very food I ate, I did not realize my dilemma. My education was financed with student loans, my lifestyle financed by Visa and MasterCard. My world would soon come crashing down, and I would not even see it coming. I thought back to my friend's days in the shoe store, with people buying two-hundred-dollar sweat suits and one-hundred-dollar tennis shoes, charging everything. My role models were Ivy League businessmen in their Ivy

League suits buying grandiose meals and paying for everything with American Express. How I fooled myself to think I was like them because I held an American Express in my hand.

I was still a dreamer. Unlike most people, I had always been an entrepreneur, and now I planned bigger ventures. Ventures fueled the surreal feeling that there was unlimited capital available just for the asking. And I did ask. I asked for an additional $25,000 in cash advances to fuel my first major business ventures. My first ventures, like most, did not succeed. I was now in debt for approximately $40,000 at 21 percent interest. I still lived rather well and believed I would rebound. Looking back, it is now hard to imagine being in debt for $30,000 at such a young age.

The point of my story is that we all have a story. To each of us who has tasted the bitter drink of debt, the story is as unique as it is bitter. We could always find some justification or reason for going into debt, and it always seems important at the time. I had a problem, a serious problem that I have successfully overcome. I could not get on the road to recovery, however, without first admitting that I had a problem and then seeking professional help. You can too. Read this book, as a start to your success. Learn all that you can during your journey. Take some of my points, add your own, and lead yourself down a path to victory and success. I learned the difference between leverage and debt. I learned the difference between good debt and bad debt and became a multimillionaire.

Wealth Note

The word usury is seldom used in today's polite society. Usury means to charge in excess. The legislature in Texas once put a numeric value on usury, defining it as charging people in excess of 6 percent interest. What happened to those days? Why has this word slowly lost use in our society?

7

Why Is Control Difficult?

○ ○

Beware of little expenses. A small leak will sink a great ship.

—*Benjamin Franklin*

Maybe you are thinking that your problems are not so severe. Maybe you are thinking you have some solution or plan to get out of debt, and possibly you do. But what you must remember is that excessive debt is really an excuse fueled by the media. As long as you are alive and watching television or going to the malls, you will be given positive reinforcement for spending in excess. Every day we are bombarded with commercials and advertisements that play on our weaknesses, our ego, and our insecurities. And if none of these direct approaches works, then sex is an effective enticement. The root of the problem, the reason so many people in this country are in such debt, lies in the very perception of the American dream. Most of the people who originally settled in America sought freedom (except slaves), and yet most ended up in debt (including slaves).

The following scenario illustrates my point about self-control. See if you fit into one of the patterns.

Don and Carey had just been married. They were in college together and had waited until they both had graduated. Now, with degrees in hand, they tied the knot and looked forward to starting a new life. The honeymoon was more than they could afford, so it was charged on Don's Visa card. They lacked many things for their new apartment, so they purchased things, a little furniture here and there, also on Don's Visa. Both Don and Carey were able to finish school with the aid of student loans, which were soon to become due now that their college days were over. Together they borrowed a combined total of $12,000. Carey was lucky and found a new job in her career immediately upon graduating. She looked forward to beginning her career as an accountant. The long commute justified purchasing a new car. This type of spending, before any money has been earned is often the pattern of someone creating debt. Since the two had just gotten married, they decided on a modest Toyota Corolla. Don was not as lucky. His job as an assistant in the computer lab ended when he graduated. And he was beginning to search for new employment in an economy that had just taken a downturn. This couple elected to start in debt and, depending on their future decisions; they may never recover from their decisions.

Credit is power in our society. That simply cannot be denied. Using a credit card sends a message to the buyer that goods and services may be purchased in virtually unlimited quantities. The buyer is an important person who is recognized by a major lending institution and is probably an upstanding member of the community. Of course, all of these things are misconceptions. The advertising media and the culture that we live in glamorize people going into debt the buy items that the conservative and shrewd businessman would never purchase on credit. This false image is one of the principal reasons that young people, especially young couples, go into debt. It is important that you do not get caught up in having the appearance of wealth as a goal. Becoming wealthy is a goal; appearing wealthy is just a cheap illusion.

Imagine how much self-confidence a wealthy person must have when they choose a humble house and modest car. In our age of fast and easy credit, young people often believe they can get something for nothing. And the something-for-nothing attitude seems to of younger generations. A correct use of credit and leveraged debt can lead to wealth. A misuse of these tools can lead to a lifetime of working misery.

The choice is yours, but you must make it.

8

Analysis of Spending and Bills

○ ○

Wealth is a measure of how long you can live without working.

—*Robert Kiyosaki*

One of the leading reasons people go into debt is the mismanagement of income. It may surprise you, but most people with debt and credit problems don't know where their money is going. I was asked to counsel a friend who was having debt problems. The following is a summary of the conversation.

LT	Hello, Chuck. I understand you are having some problems.
Chuck	Yes, the debt seems like a world on my shoulders. I am going to have to declare bankruptcy.
LT	That is pretty drastic. What percentage of your monthly income is going toward your debts?
Chuck	I don't know.
LT	You don't know? How about if I asked you some basic questions about your expenses? I think it might help.
Chuck	Sure, go ahead.
LT	First, how much money do you make after taxes each month?
Chuck	I make about $2,800.
LT	Can you list your expenses?

Chuck	Sure. Rent is $1000, my car is $400, telephone is $50, utilities are about $100, and my bills are about $200.
LT	Well, that's only $1750. What about the rest?
Chuck	There's food, $100, miscellaneous, $50. Then there are insurance and minor expenses at maybe $75.
LT	Well you have plenty left over for savings and expenses, where is the difference going?
Chuck	I have no idea.
LT	What was your total debt?
Chuck	Somewhere in the neighborhood of $85000, some of that debt, student loans.
LT	You know you cannot erase your student loans through a bankruptcy.
Chuck	Know I didn't know that.
LT	There are several types of debts that you cannot eliminate, the bankruptcy laws are different from just a few years ago, and without a clear understanding of what caused this problem, you may be headed for bankruptcy again.

This type of conversation is not unusual with someone in debt. People in debt often do not seem to be aware of the factors contributing to their plight or the elements that put them in it to begin with. Money management is usually at the forefront of these problems. If you don't know how much you are spending, controlling your spending can become impossible.

Spending Log

What I always recommend strongly is keeping a spending log. A spending log is a separate booklet, notebook, or standardized chart in which every expense, every item that you purchase, and every bill or parking ticket that you pay is recorded daily. It takes commitment to keep a written log of all of your daily, weekly, and monthly expenses. Emphasis must be placed on commitment. My suggestion is to keep a blank calendar on a piece of letter-sized paper. Carry it from work to home and write down every expense, no matter how small.

At the end of the month divide your expenses into categories, such as groceries, eating lunch out, coffee, magazines, rent, utilities, and living expenses. The more categories you use the more accurate your spending picture will become. This is the clearest method of viewing where all of your expenses are going. If you have never used a spending log before, the initial results will probably surprise you. Many times when we sit down, having come to the realization that we need a budget, we have little or no idea of our spending patterns. One of the subjects I interviewed first came to me complaining of excessive debt. When we outlined her expenses it seemed she was spending less than 60 percent of her income on bills. Her expenses (not her budget) for entertainment were less than 5 percent. A surprising 35 percent of her available funds was not properly allocated and was being lost to miscellaneous expenses, excessive waste and compounded late fees.

Today, with gourmet coffee costing in excess of $4 a cup and fast food available on every street corner, coffee and snack foods are often blamed for excessive spending. I can agree, but only to a point. If you want to save money and carefully monitor your health, do not let yourself become addicted to anything that is not good for you. Surprisingly, most addictions involve products that are not good for you. I have never heard of anyone being addicted to orange juice or walnuts. It is no coincidence that coffee and soda both of these products loaded with caffeine and targeted at consumers such as young adults and teenagers. Tobacco products are even worse in terms of the cost of the addiction and its potential impact on your health.

Beat Yesterday

Beat yesterday is actually a technique used in corporate America to track, compare, and analyze spending day by day, month by month, or even year by year. A historic record of your spending creates a pattern. These patterns can be put into definitive time periods with the goal of improving your savings and lowering your expenses by analysis of what you did yesterday. Of course yesterday can be last week, last month, or last year. There are times when corporations cannot grow due to external finance circumstances. During these times of limited or negative growth, the corporation can grow or at least maintain its income by lowering expenses. You can use the same technique.

When the real estate market stopped rising at record levels, I looked for new ways to improve cash flow. The easiest way was to lower my expenses, thereby improving cash flow and overall net wealth. I was able to lower my expenses because I had kept a record of all of my expenses for the last year in a log and could compare them. I restructured debt, consolidated student loans, and paid off outstanding loan balances with cash, thereby increasing my cash flow about $2,000 a month. I did not know that it might be twenty-four months before I was able to increase my active income, but the net gain in passive income due to early payment of my debts made a difference.

Wealth Note

The greatest freedom is the freedom to live your life in your own place and time with few worries.

9

Create No New Debts

Rich people have their money work hard for them; poor people work hard for their money.

—*T. Harv Eker*

Today I will not create any new debts.

Today I will not create any new debts. This is a strong theme in Jerrold Mundis's book *How to Get Out of Debt, Stay Out of Debt and Live Prosperously*. His work was also inspired by the proven techniques of Debtors Anonymous.

There are two levels of thought in this profound statement: it acknowledges the fact that the cure for getting out of debt and credit problems is to view each day as important, and it establishes the importance of not creating any new debt. If you have made an honest commitment to yourself to end your debt and credit problems, you must start at the beginning. It does not take a monumental effort to change your circumstances. But it does require a committed effort each day. And this will eventually allow you to achieve your goals.

Consider the example of a person who is trying to lose weight and get out of debt. Let's say the person has set a reasonable goal of losing forty pounds and clearing $5,000 in credit card debt. The person must begin to plan how the goals are to be achieved. Since setting goals is so important, it is discussed in greater detail later in the book. If you do not clearly set goals to realize your dreams, then you are simply dreaming. The human mind has the ability to achieve anything it can dream about, but dreaming is only the first step to accomplishment.

First, begin by committing the goal to writing and set a date for the accomplishment of the goal. So, for example, you could write: I plan to lose forty pounds and clear $5,000 worth of debt in exactly one year. Then you should immediately break the goal down into small attainable and attachable pieces. To lose 40 pounds in 365 days you must do two things: (1) You must not gain any more weight during the entire period, and (2) you must lose approximately two ounces of body fat per day. Two ounces a day does not seem like very much. Usually when you define goals in these terms, they become much more attainable. And to clear $5,000 worth of debt in one year, you must spend 365 days not creating any new debt. That task stills sounds hard, so let us break it down into smaller components. You must take the next 365 days one day at a time: you must not charge anything today, while you are awake. This should not be too hard, since you cannot charge anything in your sleep!

In each month you spend approximately twenty days at work and ten days at home. If you have not had the strength to cut your credit cards in half and throw them away, simply do not carry them with you to work. You will reduce the opportunity to create debt significantly. You cannot eliminate debt with numerous credit cards in your pocket waiting for the next great purchase that you simply must make. Now the goal plan seems easy, anyone who is truly serious about getting out of debt can go 60 days without charging anything, especially if that sixty days can launch $5,000 per year of cleared debt.

Not creating any new debt for the equivalent of sixty days while you are awake is just one part of the plan. If you are currently on a repayment schedule and you are not creating new debt, you will eventually get out of debt. Unfortunately, the time frame of this simple scenario can be too long if you have any other goals or desires that require credit or financial planning.

Part two of our goal to clear $5,000 in debt is even more exciting. To clear this amount of debt in one year you must consider that, including interest, this is a little more than $450 per month, approximately $115 per week. Now the example becomes clear. If you were paying off your bills by making only the minimum payment, which might only be $100 per month, you would pay off your debt eventually. But if you stop creating debt today and pay up to $500 a month toward reducing your debt, then at the end of just one-year your debt will have decreased by at least $5,000.

It is not reasonable to assume that you will be able to change your lifelong habits (good or bad) all in one effort. What is needed is an honest commitment not to create any new debt today. If you can say this to yourself, and mean it, each and every morning when you wake up, then you will be on your way to ending the frustrations associated with bad debt.

You must realize that debt is a temporary problem. It is not forever or permanent. If you start to believe your problem is permanent, it will get the better of you, no matter what type of problem it is that persists. This is why you must never lose your perspective on your debt situation. You must accept the fact that the way you feel about making debt-making purchases is the source of your problem. Most individuals get a sense of positive reinforcement from making a purchase; the negative side, the increased debt, often does not show up until one month later when the bill arrives, and by then it has become disassociated from the positive reinforcement you had in the first place. Earlier we used the example of losing weight and reducing debt. Consider the fact that the person who is overweight does not immediately feel heavier the moment they consume some fattening food. They feel the instant gratification of the food, and by the time the results are seen, there may be a general disassociation from the foods that caused the condition. The same is true of the person who is heavily in debt but still has some available line on their credit card.

No matter how large or small your goals are, you meet them one step at a time. You did not learn how to read, walk, or talk all in one day. Nor will it take you just one day to unlearn habits that may have been formed over a lifetime. Most people do not realize how their habits can lead to overwhelming, long-term debt. They rationalize each purchase, perhaps thinking this one is necessary and maybe that it is also the last item they need, and so they tell themselves they will not need to make additional purchases for some time. Another common error is to think that you will need to buy this object at some point anyway, so you might as well go ahead and buy it now, on credit. This type of thinking is usually costly and can easily add several thousands of dollars a year of debt to burden your life. Consider the burden that would result if, even though you are already in debt and make only the minimum payment on each month's purchases, you nevertheless carry this type of thinking to each of your purchases, perhaps each month or each time you make a new purchase.

Wealth Tip

If you have made the commitment needed in your life to ending debt, you must begin paying off your debts. Cut up your credit cards, freeze them in the freezer in water, take them out of your pocket. Take the first step to not using them.

Learn to live with cash. Use the American Express card, which requires you to pay off the full balance every month. You may consider using a debit card that withdraws directly from your bank account.

Before writing this book, I went through a time in my life when my debt totaled $40,000 and included no real estate. The skills that I learned in order to write this book came from a desire to survive and to flourish. I never stopped wanting to be financially successful, even during the times I was in financial misery and excessive debt. This drive, this burning desire, is a key element in most success stories. During my time of debt cleansing, I recovered financially and started to prosper. In my prosperity I began accumulating credit cards because they were offered to me at low interest rates. As an investor in real estate I valued the importance of always being able to raise cash quickly. The need to focus on the habits that got me out of debt no longer seemed relevant. I began to see some of the material results of wealth in my everyday surroundings. I drove a Porsche and a Mercedes in addition to my other cars. But one morning on the train on my way to the office, I spent nearly $100 on mail-order items before most people wake up in the morning. I knew then that I was falling back into the trap. I was about six months from finishing my book, and I thought of how it would look if I was back in debt again, trying to sell a book on getting out of debt and living in prosperity. I considered the analogy of a fat man trying to sell people a book on exercise and weight control and realized that this was not the image I wanted to convey.

If you want to help other people be successful in overcoming some of their shortcomings, it helps to have overcome the same shortcomings yourself. I decided that I needed to go on a diet. I needed to start my countdown of not spending any money on credit. I also decided that once again I needed to reduce my commercial or non real estate debt. This time my debt included some major ticket items on which I owed far less than they were worth, even though they were not depreciating. While my situation was vastly different than before, a debt is still a debt (unless it is educational debt or real estate debt) and is the worst, ugliest thing since the invention of the taxes that can plague a person and rob the health right from them. So I decided that before my book was finished, I was going to get rid of as much of the commercial debt as possible and certainly not create any new debt on a day-by-day basis. I give the analogy of a professional tennis player who studies and reacts to the importance of each shot. Although the tennis match may go on for hours, he or she knows that if they return the ball one more time than their opponent during each serve, they will eventually win the entire match. It is with the same passion that you must consider the importance of each credit card purchase. Now matter how innocuous the charge, it is leading back down a road from which you may not return. Everything that you do in your life today, every step that you take, every item that you charge moves you closer to your goals, or it moves you away from them—there is no in-between.

Wealth Tip

Think "I shall not create any new debt today" as you consider the importance of each consumer item that you want to buy, especially if you do not have the cash and you have the credit card jumping out of your wallet saying "Use me, use me!" In the long run it is not worth it.

Anthony Robbins, in his landmark book *Awaken the Giant Within,* says that the secret to overcoming any negative, self-limiting habit is to link enough pain with continuing the habit in your conscious and subconscious mind. He describes how humans live fundamentally in search of pleasure and in avoidance of pain. This model makes perfect sense of why people go in debt. They are satisfying an immediate desire by charging something or buying some item with timed payments. They feel pleasure for the moment. It is not until later, when the bill arrives, that they begin to experience some pain. There seem to be two fundamentally different ways in which people approach debt. This difference gets at the root of all debt. Person A will get the bill and send in the minimum amount of money possible on their payment plan. This gives A the pleasure of retaining their cash on hand and avoids the pain of having to pay the bill by deferring it until some later, far-off time. Person B will get the bill and pay it in full. This gives B the pleasure of knowing they have reduced a debt and will not have to pay any interest. This example illustrates the difference quite simply: person A stays in debt, while person B manages their debt and probably has very good credit. Sadly, society trains us to become person A. But all it takes is a little knowledge and discipline, and you can become person B.

Consider the words of Zig Ziglar: "no matter what you are today, you can change tomorrow." But you must be willing to make the change. Remember the motto: I shall not create any new debt today.

There is simply no other way of expressing this idea. If you have placed your signature on a credit application or car payment plan and have incurred a liability or debt, you should expect to end up paying every cent, including interest, which is stated in the total of your application. It is surprising how most people do not think that the total bottom line applies to them. A salesman may tell you not to worry about the total because part or all of the interest in some credit purchases is tax deductible, but few people actually make these deductions from their taxes. You will pay the fees associated with the purchase before you are able to deduct anything from your taxes.

Your payment plan may be slow, methodical, and progressive. But it is an acknowledgement of the debt and a plan to alleviate it. While you are engaged this plan, you must also be committed to not incurring any new debt. You must avoid the temptation of buying things to relieve the minor stresses of life. Do not spend money to feel better. Do not spend money because the weather is depressing. Do not go shopping without a reason. All too often we buy things that we do not really need just because it makes us feel better.

The people who have come to me for debt counseling are usually all too familiar with the instant gratification one gets from making a purchase.

10

The Anatomy of a Purchase

o o o o o o o o o o o o o o o o o o o o o o o o o o o o o o o o o o

I have everything I need right now to experience abundant prosperity.

—*Toni Turner*

If I could summarize the process of a typical purchase made by someone who is in debt trouble, it would probably look like this:

Stage 1. Mood. The day is gloomy, and you feel the need to cheer yourself up. Or the day is sunny and bright, and you are feeling fantastic, so you decide to treat yourself to something good, because you only live once and do not know when you will see another day this beautiful. And so you take yourself to a place where you can buy something, usually a mall or clothing store.

Stage 2. The shopper's instinct. You have decided on the item that will give you the instant gratification that you seek. If you are feeling gloomy, the item will make you somewhat happier; if your have decided just to treat yourself, it will make you feel special. You have studied the price and believe that you are getting a good deal, and you think you may not find this item elsewhere for less money. You may actually convince yourself that you have saved money by making the purchase here.

Stage 3. The rationalization. Realizing that you are in debt and should probably not create any more debt, you consider that in the grand scheme of things, the $50 you are about to pay for the item will not significantly increase the balance on your credit card. So you decide that you might even be better off if you could just purchase everything that you needed all at once (which you cannot because you lack the credit) This is a rationalization. You are using flawed reasoning to justify creating more debt. You would say to yourself, having everything

31

that you wanted and could begin paying off the debt, which you rationalize you would do in larger increments since you would not be buying anything else, having attained all of the things that you want. It may sound ridiculous, but this is actually how people rationalize this type of purchase.

Stage 4. Instant gratification. The salesperson enters your sale into the cash register, hands you a pen, and politely addresses you as Mr. or Ms., Sir or Madam, which is the first time you have heard any respect all day. (You get more respect the larger your purchase.) With just your signature and no actual cash you have the merchandise and cannot believe how wonderful it is that the country would permit this system.

Stage 5. Denial. You need to purchase a gift for someone else. And there is simply no other way, so you charge the purchase because as a good and decent citizen of society, you must maintain proper decorum.

State 6. Positive self-assurance. You believe in yourself, and you believe in your ability to manage and become successful. This small purchase is well within reach of someone with your potential.

Wealth Tip

Sometimes only moments after the money is gone, we have nothing to show for the money that we have spent. Make a habit of writing down all of your major purchases and keeping a record of them. At the end of the year you should know what you purchased and how much you have spent.

The lesson here is simple: do not shop or buy based on your emotions, your moods, your triumphs, or your tribulations. This can be a fast road to debt and poverty. This practice was also hard for me to beat. I would tie my shopping to my moods. If I was depressed, and I have suffered from depression for years, I would go shopping. But I eventually learned to shop in the grocery store or the dollar store instead of the electronics boutique or car dealership.

Next lesson: do not shop because your friends and family are shopping. These people are usually in more debt than you, and they are probably spending as much energy to keep up with you as you are spending to keep up appearances. If you want to see just how absurd keeping up with your neighbors is, watch one of my favorite British television shows, *Keeping Up Appearances.*

You cannot become wealthy by shopping. You only become wealthy by owning or controlling enterprises that create value or money.

11

Paying Off Your Debts

Riches begin with a state of mind, with a definiteness of purpose, with little or no hard work.

—**Napoleon Hill,** *Think and Grow Rich*

There are many books and many formulas for computing how to pay off your debts. Some methods make more psychological sense, and others make more numerical sense. The choice is strictly personal. The following strategy is based on those that I have read and studied over the years. It is the strategy that I used to pay off my commercial debt and the strategy that I am now applying to my real estate debt.

Many times over the course of my career, I have been in debt when I was trying to leverage real-estate and create passive income. Each time I was able to quickly resolve my debt issues, because I used a formula, similar to the one I will share with you, to minimize the interest and the duration of each loan. I accumulated a considerable amount of debt, (over $1 million), but as the real estate markets rose, and the equities that I also invested in rose, I was able to quickly mount a repayment strategy. When the value of my real estate and stock holdings exceeded $3 million, I simple redoubled my efforts to repay the loans and live off the passive income while I pursued my other passions.

This was especially important with real estate investments. Stated simply, I borrowed money at 5 to 7 percent and experienced gains of 30 to 85 percent in the Baltimore markets, according to *Money Magazine*.

I would not trade anything for the path I have taken.

—Maya Angelou

Step 1. Assess your debt. First take all of your credit cards and put them in a chart. I've provided an example at the end of the chapter. List them in order, from the lowest balance to highest, and then list your auto loan and your home mortgage.

Step 2. Design a payoff plan. You must commit to paying off your debts. You must commit to adding an extra amount per month to your debt payments, at least $50 and preferably $500. Let me show you how you can multiply the power of this additional amount to eventually take yourself out of debt. Take your amount, in this example $100. Divide your smallest debt payment by this amount; this will determine your "payoff factor." The payoff factor is the number of months it would take you to pay off your debt, not counting your regular minimum monthly payment or interest. Round the payoff factor amount up.

Creditor	Amount	Payment	Payoff factor
Visa	$1,200	$75	12
MasterCard	$1,400	$85	14

You then add this payoff factor to the payments you make to your smallest creditor. In the case of Visa, you will pay off the account in approximately twelve months or one year including the minimum payment your credit card requires, plus the extra payment determined by your payment factor. What you begin to see is that your debts can be paid off in a few years, instead of ten of years which is the usually payment schedule. With the next step we will really make this reality work for you as we accelerate the payments of your debts.

The next step is very important step. You take the full amount of the monthly payment used to pay off the first creditor and add it to the minimum payment made to your next lowest creditor. The next lowest payment is MasterCard. Your minimum payment was $85, to which you now add $175, the amount that you were paying on Visa. This brings your new MasterCard payment to $260.

This means you will be able to pay off your MasterCard in less than six months. In short, after you pay off one debt, you take the full amount that you were using to pay off that debt, plus your payoff factor, and add it to the minimum payment you have committed toward repayment of the next debt.

You may be amazed at how simple this program is. Many people have spent years trying to pay off credit cards because they have never realized that the way to break the compound-interest mystery is to pay more than the minimum and focus on paying off one account at a time.

Once again, the keys to success are:

1. Do not charge anything more on your cards.

2. Create a "payoff factor" that will allow you to accelerate the payoff.

3. Use the full amount of the old payment to pay off the next credit account.

4. Be disciplined. You must not continue to charge anything. You cannot pay off a charge card if you are still using it.

5. Include all of your credit cards, your car and your house payment if you have one. You will see this method of attacking your debts will take years off of your payments.

The problem is that the credit-card companies understand more about human tendencies, spending, and payment patterns than do consumers of credit. They understand that certain minimum payments will actually keep you in debt forever, since you will never pay off the card. Credit-card companies also know that at some point you will give up, continue to make the minimum payment, and simply open more credit-card accounts. The pain of excessive debt is this: you get to work for the rest of your life to pay credit-card companies part of your income. And in the end, the pleasures you buy—the many meaningless consumer items, dinners, watches, gifts, gas, and food—actually cost you far more than their original price. This does not make sense. By purchasing an item with your credit cards you end up paying more than its price because you pay the price plus interest on the item.

After you have paid off all of your commercial debts, add your home to the list. In many cases, depending on your debt, you will be able to wipe out your home mortgage payment in a handful of years. Compare this to the forty-year path you are currently on. The shocking reality of this simple example is that it illustrates how, by paying off your credit cards and adding those newly recovered balances to pay off your mortgage, you could pay off everything, your home, car, and credit cards, often in less than ten years.

Consider the following example.

Payoff factor   **$100.00**

Creditors	Total debts	Monthly Min.Pay	payoff factor	order to payoff	Monthly Min.Pay	New payment	Approx Months to payoff	Months to payoff
1.Chase Visa	1,400.00	150.00	14	1	150.00	250.00	5.60	Months to payoff
2. Chase Mcard	4,400.00	200.00	44	2	200.00	450.00	9.78	
3. Auto Loan	10,500.00	390.00	105	3	390.00	840.00	12.50	
4. Line of Credit	15,000.00	150.00	150	4	150.00	990.00	15.15	
5. Student Loan	21,000.00	75.00	210	5	75.00	$1,065.00	19.72	
6. Mortgage	100,000.00	900.00	1000	6	900.00	$1,965.00	50.89	

Study these numbers. This average debtor with credit cards, an auto payment, student loan and a mortgage can be debt free in less than 10 years with a marginal pay off factor of $100.00 a month more than the minimum payment, simply by adding the full amount of the paid off debt to the monthly minimum payment of the next debt while not creating new debts. Substitute your debts ir to this chart to see when your freedom date will be.

| | 152,300.00 | 1,865.00 | | | 1,865.00 | | 113.64 | Months payoff all debts |

9.47 years to debt freedom including the house

Knowledge is powerful!

Power never takes a step back.

—Malcolm X

PART II

Becoming Set for Life

12

Get a Job, Start from Somewhere, Go Up!

o o o o o o o o o o o o o o o o o o o o o o o o o o o o o o o o o o o o

The best way to predict the future is to invent it.

—*Alan Kay*

I welcome you as a new wealth-creator to your journey.

The journey to corporate America for the new wealth-creator usually begins after college. The trip could begin before college with a summer internship.

The journey to wealth is even possible without college. But learn this lesson well. Millionaires know and understand two important factors in acquiring wealth: the value of investing and the importance of long-term perspective. Your best investment will not be real estate, gold, or stocks. Your best investment will be your education. All other items can be taken from you. Governments can change; technology can render machinery and equipment obsolete. But your education cannot be compromised; it can only be expanded. If you are not willing to invest in your education, preferably through college or other formal education, you may not have the ability to recognize other investments. Second, consider the value of time perspective. Millionaires understand that financial success is not a get-rich-quick program. It is usually a get-rich-slow program. My path to becoming a millionaire took eleven years. Many people cannot finish or start college because they lack long-term perspective. They want immediate gratification. They cannot see the pot of gold at the end of their journey.

Imagine if Frederick Douglass felt that way? Douglass would not have taken the long and, at the time, illegal road to literacy. How long do you think it took for him to become a scholar and statesman, having being born into slavery? Imagine if Helen Keller had lacked long-term perspective. She lost her sight, yet she acquired vision. She lost her hearing, yet she learned to communicate in more than one language. Yet through sheer force of will and her keen sense of long-term perspective, she graduated at the top of her class and went on to become a speaker, author, and became an inspiration to many generations during and after her death.

What is holding you back?

Corporate America is filled with opportunities for the beginning wealth-builder. Many people start with summer programs, internships, or work-study during college. These opportunities have certainly increased, but they seem harder to come by for many people. But this simply does not matter. You must make your own opportunities in corporate America.

My experiences with summer internships occurred during the mid 1980s. I was able to get an interview with a large corporation, at that time a Fortune 1000 company, because a relative worked for them as a professional. This was one of my first disheartening experiences, for none of the people who interviewed me would take me seriously. I had worked all of my young life, working one and sometimes two jobs at a time to put myself through school. As a college senior with a background in computer science and headed for a degree in that field, I was quite proud of myself. Arriving early wearing a crisp blue suit, briefcase in hand, I was ready to begin my journey into corporate America. I wondered if this interview would be different because I knew someone who had already entered into employment in this company. Echoing the back of my mind was the advice "Enter quietly and sit in the back," making me nervous for the interview, but I refused to think of past experiences and focused on thinking positive.

The new wealth-creator should take note: your thoughts are projected loudly and clearly in your body language and in your speech and speech patterns. You cannot think about negative circumstances, problems in society, or individual issues, and expect to win the interview. What you think about becomes your reality. You cannot afford the luxury of one negative thought. You must focus on positive, winning experiences. To do this successfully, I encourage you to practice.

It has been suggested by numerous authors on positive thinking, that up to 90 percent of your thoughts focus on the negative things that you do not want and on your fears in life. Take this thinking into an interview and it will not matter what you say. I would later interview with an IBM subsidary. Despite sending an impressive resume and appearing professional in my dress, the receptionist asked whether it was really my resume before calling in her boss, who was to conduct the interview. I can never forget his words as he came out with my resume in his hand, looked at me, open-mouthed, and in ridicule questioned me in exactly the same words his receptionist had used: "Are *you* Mr. Tripp?" Who did he think I was? Why is it so easy for people to assume the worst in someone they do not know? My times in my interviewing for jobs, I often had people assume the worse in me, yet I never accepted this for myself. I had put myself through college and earned an associate's and a bachelor's degree, yet based on my appearance, these people were questioning whether I was the person reflected so handsomely on paper.

My interview at Westinghouse was no different. I asked questions about the job requirements and career growth. I was asked what five plus seven and two plus two equaled. I raised a point in my favor by pointing out that I had differential and integral calculus on my resume, elective classes that I had finished in college, and was again asked if I could add. I ask you: do you think this strengthened my resolve to become financially independent? Or did it make me weaker? Westinghouse is a great company with many good people, but even despite my encounter this pathetic hiring manager, I had no intention of making my future with this company. I also realized not to judge any organization for the actions of a few disparaging people.

The best job I did not get was at IBM. I still love the company, but certainly would not have retired from IBM either. I am not sure my independence would have served IBM very well. I am happier with owning their stock.

During another interview, I asked about salary; the response was: "far more than you would make at McDonald's." I had never worked at McDonald's, but from what I know, they have a great reputation for hiring properly and promoting growth within their company structure. Incidentally, The salary insult and the questioning of my basic math skills aside, I was still naive in thinking I might get some of the jobs I interviewed for. I would later realize that when an interviewer asks you such deeming questions, this was a wasted effort. I had learned from an interview with an executive at Rite Aid that some interviewers have no intention of hiring you and seem to enjoy the look in your eyes as they strive to crush your spirits, hopes, and ambitions.

Weak and useless is the manager who feels a sense of accomplishment in reporting to his or her superiors the problems, errors, and weaknesses they have found in a person seeking an opportunity. In life, there are no statues erected to critics, yet some people act as though they get paid to find fault in other people. Many people found fault in me as I progressed. Somehow I learned early on that successful people fail more than people who are considered failures. When you understand this, you will be ready for any obstacle that comes your way. Needless to say, I received none of the jobs mentioned above. While my spirit may have been bruised, it was never crushed. What sustains my success is the relentless struggle that makes life worthwhile.

Today, I do not purchase products from companies where I have met with anything less than complete respect and professionalism. I own stock in various convenience and discount stores and make all of my purchases from businesses that I feel support my interests and my community. Whenever I find my purchasing trends lead me to frequent the same establishment, I identify a stock or mutual fund that would promote my growth as I continue to patronize the company. I dine out often, and that has led to research of restaurant and entertainment-company stocks; I often stay in hotels, and this has led to purchasing infrastructure stocks. Infrastructure stocks are stock in companies that supply the same items to many hotels. Items like plumbing fixtures and bathrooms that I would notice in a variety of new hotels across the country during the real estate boom, led me to invest in certain companies, like American Standard bathroom fixtures. In many hotels, bookstores, and public places, I noticed the same company often supplied the plumbing facilities, and that led to a profitable investment in American Standard.

The Job Interview

The apparel oft proclaims the man

—Shakespeare, *Hamlet*

The interview is the first social contact that can define you for the rest of your professional and social career. The interview gives you a forum for social interaction, intelligence gathering, and sales practice in one meeting. Regardless of your skills and other factors, this is a sales opportunity. You are the product. Your audience will vote for you and pass you to the next process, or they will vote against you and end your options at this company.

It is difficult to become wealthy without being able to sell. If you cannot sell yourself, the product and commodity you know best, how you can sell anything else.

Take a class in sales if this is not one of your strongest points.

Regard each interview as a sales opportunity. Sell yourself to everyone. Start with the front receptionist or telephone operator. Often everyone who has any contact with you will be asked what they thought of you. It is only human nature. Your professionalism and courtesy are paramount and must be directed toward everyone. Speaking clearly and concisely, in a friendly tone of voice, and maintaining good eye contact are essential.

Your standard of dress must be high. You cannot climb the ladder of success wearing an outfit of failure. In any business setting, attire is a customary form of communication that encourages group interaction. Do not be excluded by dressing inappropriately. Watch the employees entering the firm and note which employees you believe are paid to work and which seem to be running the enterprise. Dress appropriately at all times, from your interview to your last day on the job. You will be judged by a higher standard. Accept the things you cannot change when playing by someone else's rules in their arena. Playing any game to win involves being successful by working within the rules, and in the case of the interview you are not the rule maker. Later, as you branch out to form your own business, people will initially decide whether to trust you based on how you dress.

One of the largest components in a successful negotiation is the establishment of rapport. Dressing like the person who will interview you is an easy way to promote and establish rapport.

Wealth Tip

A happy prosperous and successful life is truly the best revenge.

Learn to remain positive and strong. When the first ten people who interview you turn you down, you must remember to be strong and persevere. Part of what you are experiencing may not be racism. Part of your negative experience may not be sexism. Try to ease the situation by asking specific, direct questions. If you suspect that you are not being treated fairly, speak out. Let your voice be heard; you may be the only person to speak out about an injustice that has continued for years. The job market is filled with good people willing to give a person a fair chance, but it is also filled with people whose hearts harbor bigotry, prejudice, and sexism. Write to the company headquarters if you have been mistreated. Express your concerns in reasonable, objective, and positive words. Then move forward! Pursue another opportunity. You will find that you feel better for having taken an action that may assist the next person who comes along, in the hope that they will not have to feel as you did. Importantly, take action to continue the search.

Wealth Tip

Successful people have had more failures than people who are failures.

Gainful employment is often necessary to become wealthy. It is difficult to pursue financial success without the initial positive cash flow that a job can bring. Gainful employment means not just getting a job, but learning everything you can about your job and the positions that support your success. Gainful employment involves constantly and steadily growing as a person and as a business professional so that you always have more to offer your employer and, more importantly, yourself.

One of the best bits of advice I received during the employment phase of my entrepreneurial life was to be the best employee in my given field. Brian Tracy, in his book *Getting Rich in America*, clearly states that by being an expert in your field of work you will earn top dollar. Those top dollars can be successfully invested elsewhere to start your own business. I worked as a computer scientist while saving to become a real estate investor. If I had not been at the top of my field, it would have taken much longer to gain my initial investment capital. My success often produced 50 to 100 percent more income per year than my peers. The additional capital enabled me to invest sooner and with more financial resources than my competitors. If a person does not work hard and pursue their career with some degree of passion, they will probably not develop the skills or study habits they will need to become a successful entrepreneur. In this age of global business, you cannot afford to be mediocre in your career. If you start your career path at McDonald's, be preeminent in your position at McDonald's. Plan to become a majority stockholder, the top sales manager, and eventually the largest franchise holder. Seek to become employee or manger of the month and to obtain various other acknowledgements that will make you stand out among your colleagues. The majority shareholder of any successful American corporation and the president of Microsoft have at least two things in common: they are both rich and at one time they had to acquire their first share of stock. I often share with my students a story about an employee at Wal-Mart who rose from salesperson to become department manager of women's clothing. While this was not a monumental move up the career ladder, during the twenty years she worked there she also purchased Wal-Mart stock regularly. As a result of growth, splits, and value increases, she retired after twenty years at Wal-Mart with over $1 million of Wal-Mart's stock. She can now sell all of her Wal-Mart stock and live a life of luxury.

If you can rise to preeminence among the people around you, the seeds of entrepreneurial success are in you, you need to nourish and cultivate those into seeds of success.

Success produces success, just as money produces money.

—Sébastien-Roch Nicolas Chamfort

13

Education Is the Key to Success

A teacher affects eternity; he can never tell where his influence stops.

—Henry Adams

Early in my life, I planned to attend a community college to get a two-year degree, and then transfer to a four-year college to get a four-year degree, thus graduating with two degrees in four years instead of one degree. I cannot tell you how much opposition I encountered in discussing this plan with my teachers and peers at the time. The general thought was that community college was unnecessary. They told me I should try to get accepted into the best and most expensive university that would accept me. For most people this type of conventional wisdom is a mistake that often means not graduating at all. I even started school at a four-year university, under the negative influence of other people. As I had predicted prior to setting my own educational goals, it was a mistake that almost cost me graduation. By the time my second year came around, I had wised up. I transferred to a two-year community college, where I received some of the best instruction of my academic life. State community colleges often have a high percentage of PhDs teaching classes, because of their state-funded pay structure. The schools' primary focus is usually not profit and name recognition but rather the quality of the education the student receives. After graduating with honors from an MBA program, I went back to lecture and teach as an adjunct professor at the school where I received my associate's degree. Even though I am now a multimillionaire, I prefer to teach at an institution that made the most difference in my higher education.

They know enough who know how to learn.

—Henry Adams

Carefully consider my words in this area. *Graduating itself is more important than the school you attend.* Most potential employers will probably have never heard of your school unless it is an Ivy League university. The impression they have of you as a candidate for employment will be based solely on your success, not the success of other people who attended your school. I graduated from high school with a number of people who never went on to attend college because they did not get accepted into Harvard, Rutgers, or Princeton. What this does to you in the competitive job market is obvious: what type of person is more marketable, one with a degree or one without a degree? Read the Wall Street Journal Article, "Any College will do" (December 2006), which illustrates that getting to the top in business and in life may have more to do with you, than finishing in an Ivy League School.

Wealth Tip

It is more important to graduate than where you attend school.

My extended plan was to secure at least $1 million in assets from working and investing by my thirtieth birthday. After accomplishing this goal, I intended to pursue my MBA degree and teach at the college or university level part time while writing my books. Writing, however, has been one of the hardest goals to pursue because, while my confidence in all other areas has been off the charts, I have never been as confident in my writing. Often I complete draft after draft, only to be left feeling that the work is just not quite good enough.

Carefully consider this sage advice: always pursue your goals with a plan while concurrently increasing your education and your investments. If not all of your grandiose multimillion-dollar goals come to fruition, you will still end up in a place of your choosing. At all costs avoid debt that is not for education or real estate. One of the largest encumbrances on your success will be how much money you owe other people.

Wealth Tip

Each dollar in debt represents one hour of your life, compounded monthly. Do what ever you can to avoid owing your life to anyone but yourself and your family.

Grades are important as a measure of your attention level in a class or exercise. They are not important as a measure of your business success. Finishing school indicates that you have the responsibility and diligence to start and finish a long-term project. You would be wise to realize that starting and finishing school with a lower GPA is better than having a high GPA but failing to finish what you started. Grades represent someone's opinion of you and are representative of the quantity and quality of work that you could do at that time. Do not be defined by your grades, and do not let people define you by your grades. I have never heard the CEO of an investment company or a hedge-fund manager asked about his college GPA. Also note well that the winner in business is usually the person who has studied the objective the most, has the best understanding of it, and is familiar with all available options. In school, this is usually the person with the highest grades.

Many people that I went to school with would repeat a class if it appeared they would finish with a C. This enabled them to maintain very high GPAs, but many of them did not finish school due to the excessive repetition of coursework. Students who were focused on finishing, like myself, finished sooner and focused on the business elements of success that come after school is finished. In my business career I have been able to hire many people who attended school with me, many of whom finished with higher GPAs but were less focused on business success and financial independence.

Wealth Tip

The completion of your education is a necessary step toward wealth. To have education without financial security, or financial security without your education is a loss to both.

After school I realized that many of the old paradoxes I had read about in books by successful entrepreneurs were true. Students with A averages worked for students with C averages because they were the ones usually starting businesses. Engaged students viewed graduation as a step to economic prosperity and forged ahead. Many A students seemed to feel a sense of entitlement and expected to be hired for high wages before they had proven their worth. Student who graduated with C averages did not seem to have this mindset. I do not advocate mediocrity in any capacity. I encourage progress and continuous advancement toward the completion of worthy goals.

Successful people are generally not mediocre in their career, on their job, or at their school. It does not make sense that a truly successful person would be just average in every other area of their life. Bill Gates did not drop out of Harvard because he was having trouble with the coursework. Reginald Lewis did not purchase a billion-dollar corporation because he was tired of being a lawyer and thought he was not going to be a success. Of course, there are always exceptions.

Wealth Tip

One of the largest encumbrances to your success will be how much money you owe other people.

14

The Influence of Family

If you give people light, they will find their own way.

—Dante

One of the greatest hindrances to becoming debt free and set for life may be your own family. Remember these words of sage advice: people will do the best they can with what they have. If your family grew up during the Depression, do not expect them to have an attitude of accepting abundance. If your family grew up during the unrest and turmoil of the civil rights movement, do not expect them to be open and gracious to all of your liberal friends and your ideas of pluralistic consumption. If your family has produced no college graduates, do not expect them to understand your perspective on differences between private and public schools, and do not expect them to support a–$50,000 student loan. Never expect your family to understand why you are joining the military to pay for your college education if no one in your family has done so.

Wealth Tip

It is a fallacy to think that your family's opinion counts in an area where they have no expertise or real authority as anything more than just an opinion. Often sincere, often thoughtful opinions can be more persuasive than facts when coming from someone we trust, honor and respect. Make sure you do our research!

This does not make them bad, unsupportive, or naive. It just makes them people. My real-estate investment company and private-equity ventures provide an excellent living. To this day, I am certain my family has no idea of what I really do or how I acquired the property and stock in our portfolio. Nor do I believe my family in England knows what an MBA is or why I read the *Wall Street Journal* every morning. In my younger years, I may have thought they were simply not supportive. Now I realize that people will do the best they can with what they have learned from their lives and experiences. It took me a very long time to grasp this concept. I once heard two of my mother's neighbors argue about the most minor of issues regarding encroachment on one of their lawns. One neighbor used every expletive and nasty, obscene word she could muster. Earlier in my life and career, I would have said she was rude and crude and would have done whatever I could to avoid her. The reality is she cleaned other people's houses all of her life and saved enough to purchase her own home in a beautiful neighborhood. This explains why she was so upset at such a minor encroachment. Hers is a great story of personal diligence—despite her vocabulary and limited higher educational exposure—and disciplined savings. I am sure if she had the benefit of an MBA, a law degree, or even access to an educational system like we have today, her reaction would have been more suited to my limited empathy.

She expressed herself and communicated in the best manner that she could.

Wealth Tip

People will do the best they can in life using the tools they have acquired during their journey just as you will find success with your tools.

Brothers and sisters are themselves an exercise in discipline and understanding. In their book *The Millionaire Next Door*, William Danko and Thomas Stanley explain how the sibling that receives the most financial support and help from the parents is often the least successful.

According to William Danko and Thomas Stanley: if you are not one of the following: the favorite, the youngest, the oldest, the first boy, the second boy, the first girl, the second girl, or some other birth-related anomaly your success is still determined by you.

Your success will not be limited unless you choose to let your success be limited. I have counseled people who are successful entrepreneurs trying to get to the next level of success who seem to harbor an underlying resentment because their parents continued to fund a sibling. Take this advice: you cannot afford to harbor any ill feelings toward others, especially family. You cannot afford the luxury of one negative thought. In business, there is too much competition; you do not have enough time or energy to focus on what is important if you fill your mind with this type of triviality.

The opinions your family has of you are in reality no different from the opinions of strangers. If I listened to the people in my family who told me I would not succeed and looked at them any differently than people on the street who told me I would not succeed, my story would have been different. It is a fallacy to think that your families' opinion counts in an area where they have no expertise or real authority. These words of advice may make you feel uncomfortable. You may believe your family has known you longer and better than anyone else. This may be true. But human potential is limitless. Your potential is limitless. You can ponder the shortcomings that you had as a child or young adult and turn them into your strengths or you could continue to flounder because of them. The decision to do so is yours. The decisions that you make in life will affect your success more than the decisions that you let others make for you. You cannot foster mediocrity in yourself. You must take in the negative influences of other people and the world around you to remain static. Human potential is dynamic and fundamentally fluid.

Wealth Tip

You, cannot practice being a success alone, you need other people.

15

Choose Your Peers Wisely!

You can develop any quality in solitude, except one, character.

—Aristotle

If I were writing a book about sociology, I would state, with the certainty of experience, that poor choice of friends is the number one reason why many underprivileged people do not build the foundations they will later need. If I were writing a book on office politics, I would say that negative relationships formed with people at work constitute the number one reason why people do not become more successful on the job. We often form relationships, both professional and otherwise, with people whose thinking is detrimental to the objectives of the department and often the company. These relationships are often based on proximity rather than practicality or potential for success. When we look at a street gang, we see a group of people who generally live in the same area and come together with a common cause. The group is not based on the expertise, leadership, or vision of its members; it is simply an alliance of people who exist in close proximity. Business relationships are often no different and meet with the same lackluster results. The human mind seeks comfort levels and comfort zones without consideration of forward progress. Make a list each year of all of the people in your life, both professional and personal, and rank them. Next to each person on the list write whether the relationship is draining, neutral, or positive. If you have too many draining relationships, it is easy to see why you have not been more successful. If you have too many neutral relationships, then you are probably not maximizing your potential to grow through the experiences of other people.

I strongly urge you to reevaluate all of your relationships, both personal and business. Analyze each relationship in terms of what you are getting from the relationship. Does your interaction with the person make you stronger, wiser, and more in step with the achievement of your goals? Does your interaction fill your mind with complaints and problems or stories of doom and despair? Or does the relationship fill you with wonder and amazement?

Many people, for one reason or another, usually a history of frustration, diminished expectations, and learned helplessness, seek solace in the failure of others. *Do not become one of the others!* If you think misery loves company, then despair loves everyone and everything associated with failure.

Do not allow yourself to become part to this negative aspect of our culture. Do not go out to lunch with people just because they were around at lunchtime. Do not share your dreams, hopes, and ambitions with people who dream only at night and live paycheck to paycheck during the day. There is nothing wrong with these people, but they can and will steal your dreams, and if you are around them long enough, you will eventually think like them and become a member of their gang.

Wealth Tip

You are the average of the three people you spend the most time with.

You simply cannot grow if you maintain an environment of despair around you. Your decision to become debt free and set for life will take you down the path less traveled. These concepts sound strange, but consider educational studies where children have been mistakenly or intentionally placed in advanced schools and learning programs. Consider people who were incorrectly diagnosed as mentally retarded or mentally defective and raised in such an environment. How did they fare? In most cases people become a product of their environment. A child raised in a ward for mentally impaired children becomes a mentally impaired adult. A child raised in a school for gifted and talented children become gifted and talented. A person who works around the dream stealers, the "someday I will" people and the "isn't life unfair" people, will begin to see the world and life in the same limited view. You would be wise to consider the counsel you seek and the friends that you keep. Some people feel they are on a journey and have no mentors among their friends and family. I have always found the best mentors in bookstores and libraries. These mentors do not argue, they seek no emotional or financial gain, they do not borrow money, and they are largely unbiased when it comes to the people who are seeking their counsel.

If your friends are losers, say good-bye and wish them well. Remember that no one will have your dreams except you.

Wealth Tip

Independent thinkers will usually do only slightly better financially and educationally than the company that they keep. Take a shortcut to success and stay in better company.

16

The Importance of Planning

o o o o o o o o o o o o o o o o o o o o o o o o o o o o o o

Facts are better than dreams

—*Winston Churchill*

Zig Ziglar once said that "you cannot hit a target that you cannot see, any more that you can reach a goal that you do not have". The following goal formula is adopted from Zig Ziglar's formula, which he prescribed many years ago. It is still just as valid today.

- All goals must be written down. Mental imagery is not sufficient.

- A date for accomplishment must be included. Without this, you have just a dream.

- An action plan must be included. It is vitally important to list what the first step is, what is next, and so forth.

- The obstacles must be identified. There will always be obstacles to any goal worthy of achievement.

- A list of the people who can help you and who may hinder you must be written down as well. Everything that you want in this world is owned or controlled by someone else. This includes money, property, admission to college, knowledge, everything.

- The benefits of accomplishing your goal should be included in the writing. You must be able to clearly articulate why the goal is important to you. Often we confuse our goals with the goals of others. This wastes time and leads to indecision and indecisive actions.

Goals that are not written are only dreams. We all have dreams, but few people make their dreams come true. Those who accomplish their dreams first defined them as goals.

Carleton Sheets has said that "goal setting is as important to your success as the air you breathe …" in his course on real estate investing. I cannot agree more. The entrepreneur will understand this wise counsel, for all thoughts and aspirations are as yet undefined and flow like water in the ocean. Only when they are concentrated and given a direction and a purpose can they produce electricity and energy to run our cities.

Can you imagine setting sail from a port without a map, a destination, or a plan for your journey? Can you imagine getting into a cab and telling the driver to drive just anywhere and let you off just anywhere? Unfortunately, this is the path that many entrepreneurs and working people will take as they bounce around and near some of the richest ports in the richest country on earth. Without a plan, a roadmap, or set of articulated and actualized goals, they bounce from port to port, never fulfilling or completing a chosen destiny. Many people will read this and still not set goals. Many people will think that it is sufficient to have goals your head. This simply does not work as effectively as writing the goals down on paper, by hand, and posting them where you can see them. The tool of writing out your goals seems to trigger your mind to work toward their attainment. You cannot hit a target that you cannot see, any more than you can accomplish a goal that you do not have.

The more specific and meaningful your goals are, the more likely you are to accomplish them. Here is an example of a vague wish:

I want to be rich.

Here is an example of a sincere goal:

> I want to have a million-dollar net worth by the time I am thirty years old. I will accomplish this by selling exceptional goods and services to ten thousand people over the next ten years, according to my written business plan. I need to develop a network of sales professionals and identify companies that sell mailing lists in order to target customers in my demographic.
>
> Accomplishing this goal will help my family and me financially and will lead to a secure retirement for my parents and my family.

Wealth Tip

In life we choose our own path, and then call it our destiny.
—Unknown

By setting goals and planning, you can reach some or all of the following goals, just as others have done.

- Semiretirement at age forty or fifty.

- Full retirement at age thirty or forty.

- Travel from coast to coast, vacationing every year, new road trips every month.

- Purchase a BMW, Mercedes-Benz, or Porsche convertible with no car payments.

- Buy a home for your mother.

- Shower your significant other with diamond jewelry and trips to Atlantic City and California.

- Work one to two days a week doing something that you love, and vacation year round.

- Play the game of life by your own rules.

By not setting goals, this is what usually occurs:

- Live paycheck to paycheck even when you have a job.

- Hate your job, hate your boss, hate your spouse, and hate your life—even though you were the one who created all of these things in your life.

- Always play by rules set by someone else.

- Never reach a comfortable retirement age because you cannot save enough to live comfortably.

- Work each year for progressively younger and younger people.

- Spend the first three months of the year working to pay Uncle Sam and the next six months working to pay someone named Visa or MasterCard.

- Learn to live off a meager social security income in your older years, hoping you do not get sick.

If you study these lists, you will agree that the pain you encounter by not setting goals and living without a plan is greater than the pain involved in setting goals and not achieving all of them. If you are actively pursuing your goals it is difficult to be truly depressed or life frustrated if you have some goals and activities that you are actively pursuing.

> *"… if you don't get up every morning with a burning desire to do things. Then you do not have enough goals.*

> —Lou Holtz

Entrepreneurs cannot afford to leave life to chance. The basic tenet of being an entrepreneur involves failure and correction to meet success. Only by creating a flexible roadmap can you plan to overcome the adversities you will encounter.

Wealth Tip

You will encounter adversities whether or not you plan and set goals, but at least you will be better prepared if you have a plan.

Setting Goals:

This is a true personal story. I was sitting in a bookstore reading a car magazine. (I later banned this magazine from my reading list, Monday through Thursday, when I decided to spend my time more productively.) I walked to the real-estate investment section, where I saw an old favorite from my reading list, Robert Allen's book, *No Money Down*. I remembered studying this book years earlier and decided to give it another look. The first thing I did was review the copyright date. I like to do this to ensure I am reading current information. A light went off in my head when I saw the copyright date. It was about ten years ago, the same time that I began my real-estate endeavors. In the first chapter, Allen talks about how, with a ten-year plan for acquiring real estate, a person could retire and live off of the investments. I felt that I was very close to being in this position. With interest I reread words that I had first studied ten years prior as a student of real estate. I compared events in my own life, my purchases and my frustrations, to Allen's description of his entry and exit plan. I made a mental note of how quickly the last ten years had passed and thought of the disastrous position I would be in if I had not started purchasing real estate. As I write these words, the U.S. economy is quite dynamic. We have gone through the tech crash of 2000–2001, the real estate credit crises, war in Iraq, concerns with Social Security, high energy prices and companies are displacing thousands of people. The dot-com craze is now a bad reality, the subprime mortgage crunch is next; people from different walks of life speak shyly about how much money they have lost in the stock market. Enron, once an extreme highflier and a Fortune 500 company, has become one of the largest American bankruptcies of all time. Other companies are about to follow. Over speculation and corporate greed (the kind of greed that is not good) separated the executives, who lost little, from their employees, who lost everything.

An excess of ten years ago I started buying houses and purchasing stocks. I purchased two tax-lien properties for a total of less than $1,000. At the time, I realized just how little I knew about real estate or investing. I knew that I could not grow without taking some risks. I also knew that knowledge had been the key to my success in many other areas of my life, so I decided to immerse myself in studying the business of real estate. I made plans and scheduled classes to attend. I also attended lectures and conferences, some free and some for a fee. I made myself read daily, reading every real estate book I could find. I read, borrowed, or purchased everything written by the no-money-down gurus. I leaped slightly ahead of what was required to be successful in this field, but I knew that unless I did something different than everyone around me I would not have results that were any more favorable than theirs. Soon I would purchase a Veterans Administration (VA) foreclosure for less than $50,000, financed by the VA for a small down payment. That one property has yielded a positive cash flow of approximately $250 per month for nearly ten years, nearly $30,000 all told. Using Allen's description of finding gold in your own backyard, I have accumulated millions of dollars of real estate in similar neighborhoods. Neighborhoods that are less than fifty miles from my house have become million-dollar investments.

Wealth Tip

Many real estate gurus who sold no-money down real estate schemes have come and gone: some are in jail or pending trial for fraud and mis-representation. I do not subscribe to any get-rich-quick schemes. My philosophy of sound fundamental investments in a reasonably inflation-ary market will yield incremental, progressive gains in the long run. You can get rich at a moderately slow pace while others will not become rich at all.

Many years ago I was working at a job that I hated, working around people that I would not have chosen as friends. Today I work when and where I decide. I enjoy interesting projects with people who I think can help me grow personally or financially. I also teach, and I donate money to charity based on my earnings as a teacher. Three passions I developed in college were computer science and economics and finance. Now my work and lectures are centered on my old college passions. Ten years ago, I had to work to pay survival bills. I still have some survival bills, most people do, but now I work to pay off my liabilities and pay down my real estate debt a little faster. I work to add to my investment portfolio. I thought that I would be fully retired by now, but I enjoy working and contributing more than just my own financial success. My story is a also story of unsuccessful jobs, video stores that did not flourish, businesses that did not make me millions, and executive positions that I assumed at a young age and that went nowhere. I have not met my own expectations in many businesses and many business activities. But even if my business ventures were unfruitful, I continued to invest and learn more about investing. Reading Allen's book for the second time, I reflected on the many missed opportunities and gave thanks for the millions of dollars of income-producing real estate and the small stock portfolio that I had acquired. One house and one stock at a time, according to Peter Lynch's book, *One Up on Wall Street*, is all that is required for financial success.

To get you thinking about planning ahead in two through five year periods is essential. Time will pass by you faster than you can ever imagine. "The greatest gift that God gives us is the knowledge of our own mortality," according to Anna Quindlen in *A Short Guide to a Happy Life*. To make the most of time you must plan ahead, enjoying each day but always having a plan for tomorrow, just in case you are lucky enough to see tomorrow.

Wealth Tip

People will overestimate what they can accomplish in a day, and underestimate what they can accomplish in a lifetime ...

What were you doing five years ago? What were you doing ten years ago? It is possible that you may have had some of the same frustrations you have now. It is possible that you may have had some of the same debts and the same bills. I ran into an old former employer and noticed he had on the same shirt as when I worked under his dictatorship five years prior. Without planning and action, little may change over the next five years.

Change may liberate you from a life of work and making debt payments on non-appreciating assets. Change may lead to a life that fulfills your dreams. The economic system in America is set up to consume all of your earnings; credit, delayed payments, and the miracle of compound interest work against you and for your creditors. Imagine the paradox of America being a country with a very high income per capita, yet most people feel broke, under funded and live paycheck to paycheck. Every merchant, business enterprise, and lending establishment is trying to obtain as much of your present and future income as is legally possible. Only you can effectively break this pattern. Instead of going through the next five years of your life spending all of your money on transportation, housing, and other expenses, justifying your purchases as being necessary to survival, create a plan. In that plan save some part of your income, no matter what; invest in assets that may pay you money instead of requiring maintenance.

Do not fall into the trap that ensnares millions of Americans. Many people earn high incomes over a lifelong career, only to end up with one house (not paid for) and one car (not paid for), waiting to retire on the meager income of social security and a pension that may not even exist when retirement day finally comes.

17

Basic Steps for Becoming Debt Free

∘ ∘

Neither a borrower nor a lender be.

—**Shakespeare,** *Hamlet*

No person hoping for success should be without a plan for success. Someone else has already encountered most of the problems that you will encounter in life. Your goal is to find the lessons to be learned from the history of your own endeavors. What did someone else do? What worked before? What did not work?

A plan for life should include educational objectives, goals, and details. Do not just let your life happen, for you may not like the results.

A business plan should be separate from your life plan. There are many free templates available on the Internet and software programs that can be used to produce a business plan, so it is not necessary to discuss them here.

Failure to plan is a plan to fail.

—Unknown

One of the most neglected components among the entrepreneurs that I have counseled is their business plan. It is amazing how many people will plan a party, a wedding, or a weekend but will have no plan for their life, education, or goals. There are people who will make a daily to-do list for their activities yet will not write a business plan when they undertake a major endeavor. There are people who will create a shopping list for their home budget yet will not create a plan for their business cash flow or cash-from-operations statement. Usually these people do not last long in business. But why utilize the effort and resources of those around you, only to end with such a predictable failing?

As I said before, as a young man I planned to attend a community college and get a two-year degree and then transfer to a four-year college and get a four-year degree. That was my education plan. I planned to study electronics or computer science, so that I would become employable immediately after obtaining my first degree and have income that could be used to help pay for college costs.

I wrote down this plan on paper, and I set dates to accomplish the plan. I monitored my progress against my plan. I planned on starting my college career working part time; using student loans to supplement my income until I had a degree in hand and could put myself in the market for a higher salary. I learned early that success would come from following the goal-completion process.

Here is your plan for success. Add the components and modules that best suit your experience, interests, and skill sets.

Basic steps

1.   Make the decision to become financially successful.

2.   Decide to pay the price required for that success.

3.   Pay off all commercial debt.

4.   Increase value by increasing education.

5.   Start a small investing business; this can be one house, five stocks, or some other form of passive income.

Passive income, recall, is income that is produced without requiring that you actually put in personal time proportional to the growth. For example, when you go to a job you are producing active income because you are producing some income for each hour worked. Consider the person who owns a one-million-dollar portfolio that increases in value by 10 percent at the end of one year. That person has produced $100,000 of passive income without ever commuting to a job or working directly to realize the potential gain. The success of that person, who many would say was lucky, was probably the outcome of planning, desire, and perseverance.

Five Steps to Success in Summary

First, make the decision that becoming wealth is what you are going to do. Put these words in writing. Understand and believe that you can accomplish what you decide to accomplish within reason. Many people will not become rich, not because they lack information, but because they lack of knowledge.

Second, decide to pay the price required to become wealthy. For years I wanted to own a Porsche 911. For years I purchased every similar type of car I could find that cost less than a 911. This included two BMWs, other Porsches, a Corvette, and a string of other cars. Just imagine how much money I would have saved if I had just purchased a Porsche 911 in the first place? My failure to plan for this car purchase caused me years of problems and inefficiency. My failure to set the purchase as a specific and worthwhile goal caused me to become mired in indecision. Other decisions in my life were similar. I would spend thousands of dollars around accomplishing a goal of appeasement. Not really accomplishing my goal, but coming close enough to appease myself that I had accomplished my goal. The cost is that you will not enjoy what you have accomplished or even feel as good about any accomplishment as deserved.

Third, create an environment for success by identifying your outstanding debt and targeting it for termination. It is almost impossible to become wealthy while paying compound interest. If you use the compound-interest scheme against your credit-card companies, paying more than the minimum on at least one credit card, and then using the balance you have freed after paying one off to pay off another, you will be free in months instead of years. Buy what you can afford, as long as you can afford to pay cash. Do not create debt for any destructive assets. Create debt only for your education and your investments. Investments will put money in your pocket, not take money away from you.

Fourth, continue your education. This one action can be the difference between struggling with a low paying job and obtaining gainful employment that gives you the income and revenue needed to start your own business.

Fifth, learn how to invest in real estate and stocks. Invest in what you understand. If you do not understand either, you have some additional reading to do before you get started. Become as proficient in your knowledge of investments as you are in your greatest talent in life. One of my exceptionally talented home improvement friends had read many books on masonry work, carpentry, and landscaping. Surprisingly, he had never read a book on investing. He could not trace the thousands of dollars that he made doing home-improvement work and had nothing to show for it. Guess what type of reading I recommended to him first. Another example: millions of Americans eat everyday, yet few have read a book on nutrition. This seems an obvious oversight, considering the many diet-related problems Americans suffer.

Compound Interest Mystery

Say you are offered two jobs, each for twenty-five days. One person offers you $1,000 a day for twenty-five days. The other person offers you 1¢ the first day, doubling your pay each day for twenty-five days. Which job pays you more money?

Compound Interest Mystery

Day		
1	$1,000.00	$0.01
2	$1,000.00	$0.02
3	$1,000.00	$0.04
4	$1,000.00	$0.08
5	$1,000.00	$0.16
6	$1,000.00	$0.32
7	$1,000.00	$0.64
8	$1,000.00	$1.28
9	$1,000.00	$2.56
10	$1,000.00	$5.12
11	$1,000.00	$10.24
12	$1,000.00	$20.48
13	$1,000.00	$40.96
14	$1,000.00	$81.92
15	$1,000.00	$163.84
16	$1,000.00	$327.68
17	$1,000.00	$655.36
18	$1,000.00	$1,310.72

Compound Interest Mystery (Continued)

19	$1,000.00	$2,621.44
20	$1,000.00	$5,242.88
21	$1,000.00	$10,485.76
22	$1,000.00	$20,971.52
23	$1,000.00	$41,943.04
24	$1,000.00	$83,886.08
25	$1,000.00	$167,772.16
Totals:	**$25,000.00**	**$335,544.31**

This example shows how compound interest works against you and for your credit-card companies, making your creditors rich at your expense.

Wealth Tip

Albert Einstein—The most powerful thing this man of science and physics claimed to have encountered was compound interest!

Many people will cite examples of millionaires who never needed a college education to become wealthy. After I had attained the millionaire status and had several businesses with varying degrees of success, I thought I was ready to teach at the college level. What I discovered was that most successful millionaires have advanced degrees or even multiple degrees. If you are in a peer group that pushes the belief that many millionaires earned their wealth without degrees, you are probably in a peer group that has neither a higher education nor much financial success.

On my last day of class in my MBA program (I graduated at the top of my class, by the way), I was asked to teach my first international business class at a local college. When I started my financial career, I sold shoes and operated a gas pump. It was going to be much easier for me to obtain financial success as a college professor with an MBA than as a shoe salesman or service station attendant. Life is even better when you do not have to obtain financing and when you are not worried about your credit score, constantly monitoring it so you can finance your major purchases.

I recognize that personal development does not always mean working toward an advanced degree. Decide to read one book a month on success in your chosen field. Decide to read one biography a month written by someone who has overcome some of the same obstacles you have experienced in your life. If you cannot think of anyone, the bookstore is full of books by people who have overcome obstacles. Personal development can mean listening to books on tape by people who are successful and have created self-improvement works.

Our problems are man-made; therefore they may be solved by man.

—John F. Kennedy, 1963

Wealth Tip

A goal that you have not written down, a goals with no date fixed for its accomplishment, and a goal added with no chart mapped for its accomplishment, is only a dream.

Each year for a number of years I have written down my goals in this fashion. The system has brought me untold personal reward and success. I can also look back to years past and clearly measure my success.

18

Power and Money

Money is like a sixth sense without which you cannot make a complete use of the other five.

—*W. Somerset Maugham*

To function successfully as an empowered, progressive person, you must be aware of race and circumstance but not blinded by these realities. You must understand that no one group has an exclusive hold on being treated with indifference, irreverence, and hostility.

Being a black man born in England, I used to think the only people that were discriminated against were black males born in England. As I grow older, I realize more and more just how wrong I was.

All people feel some sense of difference and intolerance. The nature of a pluralistic society is such that it tolerates egocentrism and supports cultural diversity. Therefore, you must learn basic tolerance of all people and their circumstances, many of which you may not understand or be able to relate to. The important aspect is the product, service, and integrity that must always go with your name. Regardless of how people treat you, consistent integrity must be your path to success. I have encountered racism, sexism, and separatism, young-age discrimination and old-age discrimination. It simply does not matter. I am still successful, and I have never compromised my character. I am guilty of not being as understanding or as empathetic as other people. I am also continuously trying to improve myself in these areas. The words about not being able to understand someone fully until you have walked in their shoes are true, but that does not have to be a hindrance to your success. The history of black people in America is that many of their ancestors' were brought over in slave ships. The history of Jewish people is that many of their direct ancestors survived the Holocaust. The current situation of women is that there are countries that still will not acknowledge "honor killing" as murder, a practice that is intolerable and also illegal in many societies. These facts are only a small part of a larger picture. The atrocities of the past and present are only a small fraction of the richness that each culture has imparted to today's American society. To dwell on any individual episode is to miss the whole point of survival and success.

Individuals from many groups have created obstacles for me, but those same groups have also been the source of my greatest mentors. People of religious and ethnic groups that I have fundamental differences with, have taken me into their homes and helped me with my success. I simply cannot be racist, because too many people of other races have helped me, and it is my goal and destiny to help other people and their children. I suggest you adopt a similar philosophy, one that works for you.

A hungry man is not a free man.

—Adlai Stevenson

19

Class Struggle

The first and greatest obstacle to financial freedom and success is debt. Pride is a close second as a limitation to the eventual success and prosperity of the individual. These two demons drive the class struggle that so many entrepreneurs, blue-collar and white-collar workers, students, teachers, executives, and people in general will work to maintain, even at the expense of the success of their enterprise. Success does not have its roots in crystal or shining china. Success has its roots in the reality of supply and demand, of product and market. The appearance of wealth and the trappings of success do not equate to financial security, peace of mind, or longevity of enterprise. You will always be wise to seek counsel in this area. This country has become a nation addicted to credit cards. Many entrepreneurs will even finance unsuccessful businesses, long shots, and pipe dreams using their ability to obtain fast and easy credit.

Wealth Tip

Remember that the primary reason you are in business is not for what you can buy but for the profitable exchange of goods and services.

Many people seem to forget why they are in business. Your life's work should not be simply to buy a new BMW each year. You should strive to create the means for financial independence, freedom from bills, peace of mind, and the opportunities that having wealth can create. I have a couple of BMWs, a couple of Mercedes, and some other cars. They were all bought as used cars. I drive my Jeep most of the time because of the utility and extra space the jeep provides. I do not have to impress anyone. I am impressed with my accomplishments, and I know that I have made my Mother and the charities I support proud of me. The opinions of everyone else are not my concern.

Although this country provides the greatest environment in the world for people to flourish as entrepreneurs and exist in financial independence, it has become a Visa and MasterCard nation. Consumer debt is at an all-time high, discretionary income is being spent just to maintain debt, and credit-card companies have planned and executed legal ways to remove billions and billions of dollars from unsuspecting and suspecting consumers through high interest rates, fees, and the allure of fast and easy credit.

You can fall into this trap through the largely self-limited concept of pride. Pride keeps many an entrepreneur from reaching their full potential. Pride in its most pristine form cannot be practiced in isolation. You must compare yourself to others for pride to even exist in your world. Often people will begin making comparisons that simply are not valid. For example, the next time you are in the bookstore or at the library, look outside at all of the cars in the parking lot. How many of them do you think are owned free and clear, without the burden of car payments and interest charges? The answer may surprise you. What percentage of cars, new or used, was purchased without financing?

As you drive by an expensive apartment building in a comfortable neighborhood, consider how many people who live there actually earn more money that you. Why are they living in apartments you may ask? Sometimes you can obtain more prestige living in an exclusive apartment than you can living in a house in the wrong neighborhood. The question of real wealth may not come up, because the apartment or a wealthy sounding zip code can provide the appearance of wealth, even in the absence of something else that would lead to long-term prosperity. I have worked with many startup entrepreneurs who would not be seen dead driving a modest car. The fact that they had struck out on their own as an entrepreneur meant they now had to project an image of success, lest their friends and reference group have the perception that they were not successful. Note the key words here are perception and reference group. You must avoid these manifestations of pride. They can lead to the demise of your dreams, hopes, ambitions, and goals. The death of ambition is a slow and painful death. It does not come quickly like the shot of a rifle. The death of your ambitions will come from the downward adjustment of your goals and aspirations due to debt, bills, and the harsh reality of life. It is often a life that you have chosen.

Debt can and will keep you in a limited-opportunity job forever. Debt is the most destructive force in the lives of millions on this planet. Debt at first keeps you chained and imprisoned in minor jobs that have no future, and later, if you are not careful, it builds shackles in your mind that are almost impossible to break. Debt is the single largest driving force in our economy. The national debt, the foreign debt, and the trade debt are in the news daily. Personal debt, however, makes as many casualties of entrepreneurs and is pervasively contaminating. You must understand debt if you are to flourish. The entrepreneur and businessperson must understand that some debt can be used to gain advantage. The student must learn that some debt can be used to gain an education. Everyone must realize, sooner or later, that most debt is solely and singularly destructive.

Wealth Tip

If you are paying compound interest to debt collectors, you cannot earn and produce a multi million-dollar portfolio that may allow you to retire and live off your investments.

20

Victor or Victim

It is not whether you fall down; it is whether or not you get back up.

—*Vince Lombardi*

Charles Givens, in his book *Super Self,* said you could decide to be victim of your past or victor in your future. "The decision is yours fill your mind with the negative events sorrows and pitfalls that we all have and you will remain a victim locked in your past. Sadly, this is the unconscious choice that most people will make."

I used to wake up every morning to the news playing on my clock radio. I thought this was what a well-informed person who is an investor should do to stay abreast of the daily events and various markets. After Apple come out with the iPod, I started waking up to a selected recording about success and motivation. My favorite is *The Magic of Thinking Big,* by David J. Schwartz. Now I no longer wake up depressed by the day's events, but wake up instead with a reminder to maximize my time here on Earth, to dream, to live, and to help everyone that I can while reaching my goals. In this small way, I am not being a victim of the negative programming or negative thinking that used to stay with me into the afternoon. I am a victor because my time is being utilized in the manner that I choose. I can control the information and thoughts that go through my head. Those thoughts have to help me succeed not despair.

I decided what I would study in college. I decided what paths I would take in my life. I have no one to blame but myself, and I am quite pleased with my choices. People who are successful usually take the credit for both their successes and failures because they start with the healthy mindset that they are in charge of their lives. The conduct of your life should not be delegated to anyone but you.

Sadly, people will decide to think that their parents, their friends, or the difficult neighborhoods they grew up in, or perhaps some aspect of their education
left unfinished, is what keeps them from achieving their destiny and living a fulfilling life. Unfortunately, many people will decide that they are just not worthy
of riches and success and will consciously or unconsciously sabotage their own
further success and the success of people around them. Misery truly does love
company. You do not have to be that sort of company.

If you decide that your future, which starts with each new minute, is ahead of
you to win and succeed, then no matter what obstacle faces you, you cannot help
but be successful.

You will find victory in the still moments of quiet times.

Your victory will first come in thought, to be followed by action. All successes
begin with thoughts. All life began from the energy of thought. You must think
about the rewards of success, not the problems and penalties of failure, your past,
or your limitations. You cannot dwell on being a victim, even though it is all too
easy in this largely negative society to remain a victim all of your life.

Make the decision to be a victor in your own time, even if that means your life
and your times must start over today. Refuse to let anyone remind you of your
negative past. Other people's perception of your reality does not have to become
your destiny. You have the choice. You can be a victor in your future and in your
life, or you can be a victim of your circumstances, history, and environment.
Make a decision that you can live with, because the choice is yours alone.
Remember that the path you take is up to you. If up to this point you have not
chosen a path, and if you have blamed other people for your success or lack of
success, make a decision to change today and forever. Decide that from this point
on the past is the past and that you will decide and determine what role you will
take and where you will go. You will decide what you will study, what you will
eat, and where you will live. Accept nothing less than success for yourself, and
begin to feel the self-empowerment of this process.

*You will regret the opportunities you did not take in life, more than the ones
you did.*

—Mark Twain

21

Prepare to Be Lucky

o o o o o o o o o o o o o o o o o o o o o o o o o o o o o o o o o
There is always room at the top.

—*Daniel Webster*

Definition: luck is the point in time where preparation and opportunity, perhaps unknown to others, seem to intersect. It has also been described as the moment when the dreamer and the dream become one.

Wealth Tip

Vince Lombardi once noted that many people have the will to win, but lack the will to prepare to win.

Preparation is an often forgotten and overlooked ally. Preparation begins with just a thought. It can end with bringing to fruition your greatest accomplishment. The preparation that you need to begin your journey to financial freedom begins with your thinking. You must change any thoughts you have about scarcity, adversity, or the obstacles that can hinder your progress. While your preparation will be one of education and learning from the experiences of others, both successful and unsuccessful, you must not ignore the importance of your own thoughts.

Next, learn to define your success in your terms, not the terms of others. Many people live their whole lives chasing someone else's definition of success, only to find that happiness has eluded them the entire time. There are many cases of people who have become doctors, lawyers, or some other type of professional simply because that was what their family, their friends, or their significant other wished them to do. One sure way to make sure that your dreams come true is to make sure that your dreams belong to you. Your dreams must have significance and meaning for you, and you must believe that you can accomplish them. Please do not overlook this consideration.

Many people are chasing dreams, goals, and ambitions that they do not believe in or have any long-term interest in. You have only one lifetime in which to accomplish your goals, live your life, and make your significant contribution to the world. Make sure that your dreams, goals, and ambitions truly belong to you. The error of looking to someone else for your dreams is easily seen among today's youth. Many of us would agree that young people are easily influenced by peer pressure, commercials, television shows, and athletes. But advertisers and marketers also find that people who are not so young are just as easy to influence. Peer pressure does not stop at age eighteen; it can continue throughout life, leading us to chase some very shallow and unrealistic goals. Set focused goals for yourself that will have a long-term, positive impact on your life and the lives of the people around you.

In our lives, we create our own destiny by the paths we choose, the decisions we make, and the things we choose to think about. Some of us label that destiny fate, luck, divine intervention, or some other descriptive or religious term. Those of us who are successful in our lives usually take credit for that success. Yet many of us who are not successful often do not take credit for that lack of success. It is easy to look at other people on television, in the media, and around us and attribute their successes to luck, to being in the right place at the right time, or to successful parents. But logically speaking there is a direct correlation between action, success and luck. If you pursue a course of action with impassioned desire, never accepting failure as your end result, you should eventually succeed. To drastically increase the odds of being successful copy what someone else has done; you should get the same or similar results. Plan and expect to be lucky in your quests. Optimism is empowering. Luck occurs when the spark of opportunity and success come together. Usually the lucky person does not consider luck part of their preparation for success. Oddly, the more we are prepared, the luckier we seem to become. As Vince Lombardi said that many people are prepared to win, but they are not prepared to prepare to win. There are two ways to become successful. One is hard work and perseverance, the other is to find someone who is successful and then copy everything that they have done. Surprisingly, most people follow the first method. They believe that long hours and hard work will make all of the difference in the world. Depending on your circumstances, this may be true. Reality for me came in finding someone who was successful, with a similar background, problems and obstacles, and copying many of the things that they did to succeed.

> *The reality of my life experience is that you become what you think about. What did you think about today? Did you think about a lack of money, problems paying bills, an ongoing unsuccessful relationship? Did you think about today being the first day of the start of something big in your life? Did you wake up and expect good things to happen to you all day? Or did you think that was not realistic and expected instead that today would be no luckier than yesterday? Your experiences cause you to prejudge how you look at the future. You must create a sense of positive self-expectancy in your life. You must always expect to be lucky, successful, and prosperous. To expect anything less can be a self-fulfilling prophecy.*

Early in my career I delayed purchasing a large home, much to the dismay of my parents and several of my friends. I lived alone in a five-bedroom house on one acre of land and did not have a formal job, yet many other people, some significant to me, felt my house was too small for someone with my success. At that point in my life, I had to ask whose goal was it to purchase a large home for a single person. It is true that I wanted to move and had occasionally dreamed of a big house, but my goals and dreams belonged to me, and were planned by me. My path from humble means to financial independence had not been an easy one. I had not finished my MBA at the time, and I was not in a position to purchase a hotel or office building, as had been my plan. My goals clashed with what the people around me wanted. This caused me considerable stress, until I realized what was happening. I was allowing myself to succumb to the goals, dreams, and ambitions of other people. Not until I regained my perspective could I even feel good about my own success. Do not let other people decide how your image of success should appear. Do not let people categorize you or your place in life. The most wondrous success in life will come when you find your own place in your own time, defined by you. Other people can influence you, cajole you, motivate you and support you, but you must reach the stars from your own steam. Remember that your spirit will soar only when you allow it to soar. Grant yourself this freedom, and prepare for the luck that will follow.

Wealth Tip

Since you usually get in life what you expect, why not expect the best of what life has to offer.

22

Practice a Win-Win Strategy

o o o o o o o o o o o o o o o o o o o o o o o o o o o o o o o o o

No man can sincerely help another, without helping himself.

—*Emerson*

A win-win strategy is best described as a negotiation or business deal where all parties emerge happy and feel a sense of gain from the outcome. This strategy is often talked about and written about but in practice often seems elusive. For example, after discussing the benefits and values of real-estate investments, one of my students expressed his desire to become a slumlord. When I asked him how this could possibly be a win-win scenario, he was quiet. People do not want to live in slums. Providing people with substandard living at any cost is simply wrong. The golden rule applies here. Treat other people in business as you would want to be treated.

People want decent, affordable housing. This is universal, not just in the United States but everywhere. Providing for this need can creates a win-win opportunity for you, the investor, and someone who may not be as organized as educated, or as prepared as you. People want to own something, to put their name or personal touch on something. Renting to people without the possibility of ownership does not create a win-win scenario. If you rent with the plan of someday selling the house, you may not maximize your profits, but you may well be creating an opportunity for someone else to gain in the appreciation of an asset just as you have gained. That is the concept of the win-win strategy.

My post office recently began selling stamps at a price that was higher than their face value. The stipulation was that the excess in the cost was being donated to the breast cancer foundation. I thought this was an excellent idea and told everyone in my organization that we would now purchase these stamps. This is a perfect example of a win-win scenario. We have to mail letters anyway, and now part of the cost will go toward the fight against cancer. We are not minimizing our expenses by paying more for the same service, but we are maximizing our position as business people who contribute to our society.

Examples of win-win strategy:

The following are three simple examples of property acquisition or sales using the win-win strategy. In each case consideration must be given to the other party in the deal. Success in the win-win is defined as successful business deals were each side feels that the outcome was successful to them, and the other party.

A Win-Win Purchase of a Model Home

Once when looking at a model home, I asked the builder how much they wanted for the model. My intent was to rent the house for eighteen months and then sell it, just as I do with all of my houses. The difference is that this was a new house in a new development. The rest of the houses had not even been sold. The builder, sensing that this was a potential win-win for both of us, asked me to explain in more detail the deal I was tailoring to suit both of us. I proposed to purchase the model home at the same cost as the other homes, but to include all of the paint, decorations, and other amenities that made it stand out from the generic units that had been finished at no additional cost. I proposed to close quickly within forty-five days and then rent the house back to the builder for as long as they needed it to show to potential customers. This deal benefited the builder, in that it guaranteed the sale of the model. And it benefited me, in that it would actually give me positive cash flow immediately as well as the potential to sell the house (after the last unit was sold) for a slightly higher price, since models are usually professionally painted and decorated. And in the interim, I had a good commercial tenant.

A Win-Win Real Estate Sale

Here is an example of how to create a win-win deal on the sale of real estate. Make sure that you check with a local realtor to ensure that the practice of creating a leasehold estate is sanctioned by your jurisdiction.

Lower the price of your investment property that is for sale by selling it as a leasehold estate (provided the laws in your area allow this type of transaction). Then create a ground rent on the land the house is on. What you have done, in effect, is create a potential tenant, since you are selling the house, but only renting the land the house is located on. This type of arrangement is more prevalent in older cities than you might think. Many properties are sold with ground rents; in all cases, the tenant can continue to pay the ground rent or redeem the ground rent and take title to the land. The win for the new owner, is that the house should be initially cheaper to purchase and perhaps easier to finance. Provide the new owner with a redemption contract so that they may purchase the ground also at some point in the future.

A Win-Win in Leasing

There are many ways to create a win-win situation in leasing. I have mentioned the purchase option as one method of increasing the odds that your tenant will maintain the property. You can also create a discount for early or on-time payments instead of charging late fees. After a tenant has rented from you successfully for twelve months, agree to refund part of the security deposit. Send thank-you cards or holiday cards that are nondenominational, non-religious, and non-political. Send your tenant a birthday card, or buy them a humble house-warming gift. When you receive payment of the second month's rent, send them a gift certificate to a home-improvement store for $10 or $25.

Determine that in all of your business dealings you will be honest and practice a win-win strategy. Make sure that all of your business dealings with people are mutually beneficial. You should never leave a negotiation or close a deal thinking that you have won at someone else's expense. Instead, practice the win-win strategy. You win, too, when both you and the other party feel success. Investing in real estate will invariably put you in a unique position of having control over other people's lives. Always remember the golden rule in application and as practice. In some cases, you will try to purchase properties that other people are about to lose due to unfortunate circumstances. In other cases, you will consider renting your property to people who have made some credit mistakes in the past, been through divorces, or perhaps had medical problems whose costs have impaired their ability to purchase a home. If you are in this business long enough, you will see many scenarios that could easily become your own scenario. Many landlords and unscrupulous lenders are waiting to take advantage of these people with the lures of easy credit, low payments, and other promotions. You do not want to ever be perceived as someone always looking for a way to get a new tenant. Setting standards for yourself and your company not only benefits you, it also benefits everyone who does business with you and everyone who supports your activities. The win-win strategy is the only strategy. If people perceive that you are honest with them, they will usually reciprocate. If you are genuine in trying to get them into one of your houses for a reasonable deal, they will not see you as the stereotypical landlord waiting to take advantage of the unsuspecting renter. You should realize that your tenants are paying off the mortgages on your houses. They are making you rich, one payment at a time, and one house at a time. You are the one who ultimately benefits from the relationship that you have with the people who move into your properties. Treat everyone with dignity and respect and never forget that your customer is directly responsible for your accumulating wealth.

Forget your customer and your competition will remember them.

—Unknown

There was a time when I had bad credit, high debt, and low income. When my lease terminated, my existing landlord would not rent to me and I was forced to find a new place to live. To my surprise, no one else would rent to me because of my credit history. Eventually I used a win-win negotiation to convince a homeowner to let me rent his property. I agreed, but only with a purchase option on the property. I would agree to pay the full price for the property if I elected to exercise the option in two years. The two years gave me time to clear my credit issues, establish some new creditors with excellent payments, and put myself in a better negotiating position. The landlord won because he had in interested renter motivated to keep the house in shape. I won because where I could not rent an apartment; I now controlled approximately $100,000 worth of real estate within five miles of Baltimore Harbor. A win-win strategy is practical and effective. Today, I own over $3 million dollars of real estate within twenty-five miles of that house.

In the end, no matter how wealthy you become, you will probably judge yourself by the opportunities you created for other people.

We make a living by what we get. We make a life by what we give.

—Winston Churchill

23

Commit to Saving 10 Percent of Your Income

The wisdom in this chapter alone can change your entire life, set you along the road to success, and form the basis for the continued success of your family. Does this sound too incredible? Consider the following example simplified for readability.

Medium annual income for a family	$40,000
Average number of years spent working	40
Total lifetime earnings	$1,600,000

$1 dollar a day saved for 45 years assuming 15% interest will amount to an excess of 2 million dollars according to: www.calculatorweb.com.

$1 dollar a day saved for fifty years with no interest, will amount to an excess of 18 thousand dollars according to: www.calculatorweb.com.

The lessons are clear, you must save money and you must invest your saved money.

If you are paying debt through credit cards, you are not being paid this interest, you are paying interest, often at a rate exceeding 18%.

The money that the average American earns in a lifetime will largely be spent on depreciable consumer goods and services. But if you saved just 10 percent of that money until the age of retirement, the miracle of compound interest would have an overwhelmingly positive effect on your bottom line.

While it is certainly true that many people say they cannot make ends meet and wonder how they are ever going to save 10 percent of what they make, they are exacerbating the problem. If you cannot live on your current income, a 10-percent or a 5-percent deficit will not make much difference. You are in a situation where you need to reconstruct your financial model and plan. You are kidding yourself if you think that you cannot save anything. I have known people who started saving as little as $1 a week. That small amount of money, if compounded in a safe investment or bank account, can give you some peace of mind. Imagine that if you had saved $1 per week for the past fifty weeks, you would already have at least $50 right now. Surprisingly, I have counseled many people who could not place their hands on $50.

Wealth Tip

Most people do not have a financial plan. They have no idea of where they are going. Yet they have an uneasy feeling about their future. They keep hoping that things will get better, or maybe they dream of winning the lottery.

The reality is this: without a decent plan, you are virtually unprepared for any obstacle or problem that may come between you and your success. Take some time to plan where you expect to be in the next five years. Include how you plan to get there. For those of us not born rich, a financial plan can be the guiding light by which all advertised get rich quick schemes fade. It is important to have a plan, update it often and write your plan down. Announce to other people that you have a plan, but share it with no one. This is not a contradiction. You can announce to the world that you plan to get out of debt and become wealthy without giving the details of your plan to people who may try to ruin your plans through a lack of support.

Many people get caught in the never-ending trap of spending 110 percent of what they make each year, supplementing their income with credit. So even if they are doing better by earning more money each year, they are actually going deeper into debt by a factor of 10 to 20 percent a year. They are spending all of the money they can earn and borrow each year. This is a mistake and a tragedy in the making. The middle-class rat race is a problem for many people in America. As they progress in career and in salary, they incur more debt in order to surround themselves with the consumer trappings they now feel their success warrants. Do not fall into this trap, for you may never recover. You cannot become wealthy until you start saving your money, living comfortably at or below your means, and getting rid of your debts.

Every person in society is manipulated, virtually from birth, into a pattern of creating debt. Every bank, financial institution, and credit organization sees the American public as an untold number of little consumers that need to be taught what brands to buy, how to shop, and what their values should be. Do you disagree with me? Notice how you seem to wear the same clothes, drive the same cars, and enjoy the same hobbies as other people in your reference group. Do you think this is an accident? Retailers learn that consumers develop brand loyalty early in life and tend to stay with those same brands for most of their lives.

Eventually you may come to the realization that you cannot live your dreams and live in financial freedom if you have excessive consumer debt. When you come to this realization, you may stop creating this type of debt altogether. Your purchases may focus towards appreciating items, not consumer goods that do not appreciate. One of your first epiphanies is that when you work to pay off your debt, you are working to pay off items that you may have actually purchased years ago. Many people never actually own a car because they are always making payments on the car in their driveway, which is owned by some bank. When they get close to paying it off, they purchase a new one and start the debt process over again, owning nothing and paying everyone. Many people believe their home debt is good, but then they purchase a new and bigger house every seven to ten years. Once again, they never own their house because during the first ten years of each mortgage they are largely paying interest and financed closing costs. They trade up hoping that their tax breaks will increase, but they do so at the expense of any equity they may have accumulated. The actual pride of home ownership is easily lost. When there is no increase in home equity, just prolonged debt, the American dream can become flat.

Many people live their whole lives being told what is important to them, what kinds of goals to set, how to dress, and even what mate they should choose. People fall for this. Keeping up with the Jones's, however, is a waste of effort, because the Joneses are in debt! You will also be in debt if television creates your model of success. The plan to keep you in debt and continue extracting interest payments from you is now a feature of our society. Visa and MasterCard have financial obligations to their shareholders. These obligations, along with their new office buildings and new advertising campaigns, come at your expense. The promotions come in the form of low-interest transfers, zero-interest car payments to start, or free financing for the first two years; these and other promotions will entice you to use credit to finance your lifestyle.

> The question for all of us is when we are going to die, not if we are going to die.

The problem is that your life and your lifestyle are finite, along with the money that you will make in your lifetime. The plan of the financial institutions, however, is infinite. Long after you are old and no longer on their radar, your credit institutions will find someone younger to manipulate. The banks and credit-card companies will find someone who is beginning their financial career, someone who is willing to work the rest of their life to pay off debt at compound interest.

In your teenage years, all you think about is your first car and going to school or work. You do not think that someone is looking at you, expecting you to earn more than $1 million in your lifetime and planning how they can separate you from your hard-earned money. In your twenties, you are just trying to survive, and you have started the process of trying to be like your reference group and the people that you look up to. In your thirties you are in the middle of the rat race with your spouse; or, worse, you are seeking a spouse and must have the requisite material possessions to capture that significant other.

In your forties, you now have the appearance of wealth often masked by a sea of debt. You worry about the debt, but you are driving the right car, and with your next move you will be in almost the right neighborhood. By your mid-forties, many of the dreams you had as a child and young person are starting to fade. Your energy level drops. You realize that you are not headed for a million-dollar retirement because of debt; your job seems to have peaked; and you still have not come up will that million-dollar business idea that will catapult you to success and a six figure income. This scenario can become depressing. Life does not have to advance this way. You have to realize what you want now and work to achieve it.

One day I realized I was working for freedom, not material possessions. Freedom is being able to do what you want to do in your own time frame. Freedom means you go to a job that you love, if you work at all, because you enjoy what you are doing. Freedom means deciding what car you want to drive in the morning, selecting among several cars, all paid for. Freedom means ordering lunch from the menu, instead of off the wall. It means eating good, healthy foods that you choose not because of price but because you want to be around for a long time to enjoy your family, friends, and freedoms.

My life changed when I realized what I was working for. Fortunately, I have never looked back. I would rather have 911 free days than a Porsche 911. I have experienced both. I would rather watch the sun rise from the window of my own humble home office than the beautiful downtown harbor View from the top floor sales office in a job I hated. I would rather take my Mom out to lunch than sit through another power lunch. You can have both and you can have it all, but you do not grow in your life by staying in debt. Learn how to pay off your debt, invest wisely, and save money.

24

Write the End of Your Life Story

o o o o o o o o o o o o o o o o o o o o o o o o o o o o o o o
Every man dies ... but not every man lives.

—*Tony Robbins*

Talk to an optimist, and they will tell you about plans they have for the future. They will tell you what they are going to do, where they are going to travel, and what they are going to have. Talk to a pessimist, and they will tell you where they have been, how good things were in the past, and why so many new endeavors will be difficult now that times have changed. Ask an optimist where they are going, and they will tell you how, through their efforts, they are going to get there. The excitement in their voice will rise; the energy level in their eyes will start to brighten. Ask a pessimist the same question, and their answer will depend on the economy, other people or events, and things they may have no control over.

Optimism is empowering. Pessimism is terminal. Given a choice, many people consciously choose to be pessimistic because they feel their disappointments will be lessened. Can you imagine going through life hoping that your disappointments will not be too great? A simple example is Thomas Edison's approximate ten thousand attempts to discover the filament to use in the electric light bulb. Given the enormous impact of his discovery; Edison's greatest disappointment would have been to come so close and yet not discover the process that he wanted to create. Leonardo da Vinci's biggest disappointment would have been to not pursue his career as an artist because other people told him he had other talents. Nat King Cole, possibly the greatest singing voice of his era, was a piano player until he was faced with the possibility of not getting paid for his performance when the stage singer did not show up for work. In an earlier chapter, I advised you to dream and to work for your dreams as though your life depended on it, because it does. If you are still not convinced, read the obituaries in your local newspaper. They are filled with people who had all of the problems that you do plus one, death. The time to pursue and fill their hopes and dreams will not come. You still have a chance. You still have time.

Make this day the one-day that you lived to see, the day that started a birth of optimism in your life.

> **Wealth Quote:** *Money is not everything, if you have enough of it.*
>
> —Malcolm Forbes

So many people fail to plan; they live their lives in frustration and go to their graves with their hopes, aspirations, and dreams lying dead with them. While they were alive, many of these same people would refer to events in their life as their destiny. It did not seem to matter that they lived in the freest society on the planet during the most prosperous time in all of history; these people felt helpless when it came to creating their own path in life. They ascribed their circumstances, disappointments, and tribulations simply to fate. Imagine that! Accept the challenge that life gives you to succeed.

You, however, certainly do not fit this mold. You may not be an optimist yet, but you are certainly no pessimist. If you woke up today to read this, then optimism is beginning to surface. Many people did not wake up today. They did not live to read. No matter what your circumstances today, you can choose to change them. The world is filled with examples of people who changed and moved forward in a positive direction to help themselves, their family, and their community. You are no different. Sometimes all it takes is a little creative planning.

> **Wealth Quote:** *Imagination is more important than knowledge.*
>
> —Albert Einstein

Try this exercise. Pretend that you are writing a fictional account of your future life. Use your imagination. Write in words on paper how your life will flow, what you will do, where you will live, and so on. Life is not just a combination of luck and opportunity. Life is also a blank novel, an empty notebook, and a blank chalkboard. You have the ability to create history, to make your own destiny. You are truly no different than a ship bobbing around in the ocean with other ships. Some ships have no rudder and no sails; they bob aimlessly until they accidentally hit the rocks or drift to rich and wonderful shores. Some ships drift aimlessly about until they sink or rot of old age on the sea. Other ships seem to have charted a course from the beginning of their time in the ocean and know exactly where they are going. We call those ships the Beethoven, the Mozart, and the Leonardo da Vinci ships. Your ship is no different. If you decide today that your ship will have a rudder then you will guide it to the best port available; or you can drift hoping to drift to a successful port. The choice is yours.

Wealth Quote: *I have never known anyone to be truly depressed who had written down and was pursing their goals and dreams.*

—Zig Ziglar

Describe your final port of call in detail, full of all the glory and wonder you can imagine your life to be. Include in your words of fiction a resolution to live each day moving in a positive direction, no matter how fast or slow, toward experiencing the richness of the seas. Every day is an adventure. Every day at sea brings you wonders of life that were unseen by you just the day before.

Now comes the hard part of this writing exercise. Write down ten steps that you will have to take in order to end up living the life you just wrote about. After each step, write down the first thing that you must do to move in that direction. Your journey has begun.

Wealth Quote: *The secret of getting ahead is getting started. The secret of getting started is breaking your complex overwhelming tasks into small manageable tasks, and then starting on the first one.*

—Mark Twain

As I write this chapter, America is about to remember once again the tragic events of September 11, 2001. The shock of that dreadful day as thousands of innocent people reminds us that life is precious. Each of us who by the grace of God lived through that event was profoundly touched. As we considered the lives that were lost and the spirit of humanity that prevailed, the days that followed were cherished just a little more, and arguments with friends and family became a little less important. You have the ability to plan, to dream, and to hope. If September 11, 2001, teaches us anything, it is that hopes and dreams should never be taken for granted.

There are none so blind as those who will not see.

—English Proverb

25

Consider Your Future One Investment That Can Payoff Big!

○ ○

The next $500 you work for may be the last you have to work for, if you invest that money in the right thing.

—The Author

As you reflect on your current or future home today, imagine the future. Imagine that one day, in twenty years or so, your mortgage has been paid off; after a couple of moves, you and your significant other have finally found a neighborhood and a residence that suit you, and you have little interest in moving further up or going through the mortgage hassle again. It may seem like this goal is a long way off, but consider what you were doing ten years ago and how quickly the time has passed.

If you have paid off your mortgage, you now have an extra income of approximately $1,000 per month. Now imagine that you had paid off your mortgage much earlier, perhaps in only five to ten years, because you doubled up on some of your mortgage payments and applied your tax refunds to the reduce the principal. Consider that you had also purchased a second house when you purchased your primary residence.

Now you have put up with the ups and downs of being a landlord for ten to fifteen years, plowing all of your profits and positive cash flow back into your investment. But consider your position at the end of the same time period. Paying off your house yields an extra $1,000 per month, and your investment house, also paid off, yields an extra $1,200 a month because rent has been increasing even though your monthly payment remained the same. You now have an extra

$2,200 per month to use at your discretion, which amounts to $26,400 year. This is a tidy sum to add to your retirement income, social security benefits, or income from other investments. You may even still be active in the workforce. The problem with this scenario is that few people see the big picture. We are so conditioned into spending 100 percent of our income that we often miss opportunities.

Financial experts and people in the media tell us to take out a mortgage on the biggest house we can afford, for the longest period of time we can afford. I know people who have a house so large they can barely afford their mortgage and have no other money to invest in anything. In each case, after some considerable discussion they agree that they may have been better off buying a smaller house, since that would have allowed them to invest in a rental property or stock portfolio. Having no cash means that no matter how good the opportunity that comes along, you will be excluded.

While you might possibly land a large, million-dollar contract in your working life, it is more likely that you could build wealth by saving or investing some of the millions of dollars in wages that the average Americans earn during their working life. The universal question is where does it all go? Much of that money will go to purchase items that do not benefit you, so it is important to consider investments that will benefit you both now and when you retire. Your plan for success should incorporate a worst-case scenario. My plan to acquire a million-dollar portfolio was based solely on my real estate investments. If all of my businesses failed, if I did not get huge job contracts, if the stores that I started failed, still, within a reasonable amount of time, my real estate investments would leave me a portfolio worth at least $1 million.

One real-estate investment can give your family financial security for a lifetime. As you pay off the mortgage you are developing equity in a fixed asset. That asset can become collateral to borrow enough money to start your own business or begin a future in investing. Most of the millionaires in America are still created through property ownership.

Property gives you a tax shelter during the period of time you are paying for it. If you are similar to many Americans, your taxes are high and your tax shelters are low or nonexistent. This is one of the many incentives that Uncle Sam gives you to become and remain a property owner. When you die, you will have an asset to leave to your children. This will help them become part of the financial community that is growing in America, even though it may have missed you. Real estate can become a fixed asset to borrow against for a college education, generate positive cash flow if rented out, and provide shelter and a safe and stable environment during periods of unemployment or underemployment if it is paid off. With all of the many benefits that a house or piece of real estate has to offer, imagine if you had two properties. The effort is not doubled but the benefits can be more than doubled. This level of ownership is where you really begin to act, think, and feel like an investor, and thus enjoy the benefits. For those of you still contemplating the purchase of your first house, there is little to contemplate. Since your house may be the best asset that you ever purchase, it can be a critical mistake to delay the purchase of this asset. Delaying the purchase of a house until you are reasonably economically stable is realistic. But delaying the purchase of a house indefinitely is simply not wise, according to most financial books and experts on personal finance and wealth.

Wealth Tip

Assets are tangible items that actually produce income. Do not confuse expensive watches, cars, and jewelry with real assets such as investment real estate, stocks, and bonds. If you cannot see income coming from the ownership of an item, it is not really an asset.

A common error that new wealth-builders make is to assume that many of the items they have purchased are assets. Assets put money into your pocket, consumer goods often require maintenance, insurance, a place of storage and seldom put money back into your pocket. Even the rare appreciating consumer good only puts money back into your pocket when it is sold. I have a fine watch collection. In the years that I have been collecting watches, many of them have appreciated in value. I have only made money on one of them once, a gold Rolex that I purchased on lay away from a jewelry store, and sold to purchase a more expensive one two years latter. The rest of my watches have to be stored, insured and maintained. People often justify a purchase by thinking they are buying an asset, when in reality they are only enhancing their lifestyle. These types of purchases almost never increase a person's net wealth. Our definition of an asset must be clear and honest. If the item that you are considering does not increase your wealth and takes energy from your life instead, it is not an asset. In most cases the items you once labeled, as assets could not be sold for what you paid for them. If your purchase actually decreases your wealth, it is the opposite of an asset, what is commonly referred to as a liability.

Wealth Tip

Stocks produce income from dividends and value increases. Bonds produce income through yields. Rental property produces income from rental payments and can lower your tax liability.

Clothes, cars, jewelry, and other such items produce no income and often cost money to maintain.

26

Your Goals, Specific and Meaningful in Five Years

o o o o o o o o o o o o o o o o o o o o o o o o o o o o o o o o o o

The secret of success is consistency of purpose.

—*Benjamin Disraeli*

Approximately ten years ago, I was working at a job I hated and with people I would not have chosen as friends. Today I work when I choose; basing my choice on interesting projects that bring me into contact with people who I think can help me grow. In the past I worked to pay the bills of survival. Now I work to add more money to my investment portfolio or to help the people I am being paid to teach. I thought that I would be retired by now, but why stop doing the things I enjoy.

The aim of this chapter is get you to plan your future five years at a time. What were you doing five years ago? What were you doing ten years ago? Without action on your part little may change between now and five years from today to liberate you from a life of work and debt payments. The economic system is set up to consume all of your earnings; credit, delayed purchases, and the miracle of compound interest all work against you. Only you can effectively break this pattern! I started the ball rolling down the path to my success ten years ago. I took action by reading and studying a new area of interest to me, real estate investing. I took action by making a graduated, calculated leap into buying my first investment property. I had not learned everything I needed to know, and I certainly made plenty of mistakes on my way to becoming a multi-millionaire investor. There was even a time when the generous money I made as an investor slowed down my hunger and drive for financial freedom. I bought Porsches, BMW's and a Land Rover instead of reinvesting and paying down debt. No person is perfect!

But consciously or unconsciously, I started down the path to a ten-year plan that is still with me today. I smile when I think of where I might be in another ten years. The future is yours!

> *If you give people light they will find their own way.*

> —Dante

What are your plans for the next five years? What would you like to explore? How much financial and personal freedom do you think you can gain? Five years will come and go in the blink of an eye.

Use the following plan as an outline. Modify it to suite your circumstances. This outline can be the framework of a reasonable plan for your success.

Time will travel by you faster than you can ever imagine. You must take action, starting today with the writing and planning of your goals, dreams and ambitions.

Year 1

The aim of this chapter is to get you to plan your future, five years at a time

This is the year for you to set the foundation for your success. Your focus this year will be education. Begin to believe in your ability to be healthy and wealthy in America. Think positive thoughts at all times and begin to mold your future.

1. Read and study two books on real estate.

2. Take a course on real estate.

3. Subscribe to the *Wall Street Journal* or another investing publication such as *Money Magazine* or *Kiplinger's*. Read every issue.

4. Identify zip codes as targets for property acquisition within fifty miles of your home.

5. Study government property foreclosures.

6. Learn how to make minor improvements (painting, carpeting, and other repairs) by reading and trying out your skills in your own home.

7. Run an ad for a handyman who can work by the hour. Find a system for obtaining handyman referrals.

8. Learn the various types of housing architecture: Cape Cod, duplex, colonial, etc.

9. Devise a plan to pay off creditors using the system described in this book.

10. Purchase one property at 10 to 20 percent under the asking price by the end of the year.

Year 2

You are now entering the second year of a program that has the potential to change your life. It is now time to focus more on the details and the salesmanship required for success. You also want to continue educating yourself.

1. Read and study more books on real estate and mortgages.

2. Attend an investment seminar, but buy nothing there.

3. Learn about sales and marketing.

4. Study credit and credit management.

5. Take a continuing-education course in nonfiction writing at a local college.

6. Study how real estate investment trusts (REITs) work.

7. Find one REIT to invest in.

8. Learn how to track its progress.

9. Update your 401(k). Start one if you have not already done so.

10. Consider maximizing your 401(k) contribution.

11. Use money from debt payoff in the first year toward paying off another debt.

Year 3

1. Read and study about real estate renovations and rehab work.

2. Track your REIT.

3. Find out how dividend reinvestment programs (DRIPs) work.

4.   Identify a potential DRIP company or stock in the area you have targeted for real-estate purchases: McDonald's, CVS, etc.

5.   Use money from paying off your first two debts toward your investment account.

Year 4

1.   Track your REIT.

2.   Consider purchasing stock through your DRIP.

Year 5

Establish a goal for the value of your accumulated assets, for example:
A cash flow of $14,000 per year generated by a property that you initially purchased for $125,000 at $25,000. Assuming 5 percent annual appreciation ($7000 per year), the market value of this property is approximately $160,000. Add to these one hundred shares of a real estate trust fund, and one hundred shares of a DRIP (dividend reinvestment program) stock.

Repeat the process of reevaluating your portfolio and increasing your procurements on an quarterly basis each year. During good years, add to your real estate. During bad years add to your stock and DRIP accounts.

Do you realize that by putting this simple five-year plan into action you could be set for life? Without fear of a cash-poor retirement, you could retire a millionaire. Imagine what you were doing five years ago. The difficulty in accomplishing our goals is viewing where are starting and where we would like to end up as being so far apart that we do not make an effort to progress. Consider the largest step is always the first step towards any goal. Your first step may have been to read this book, or meet with your spouse to discuss your future plans and how to get there. Your first step may have been as large or small as just to make the decision to start.

> *A man will overestimate what can be done in a day and underestimate what he can do in a lifetime.*
>
> —Unknown

27

How to Profit from Real Estate

o o o o o o o o o o o o o o o o o o o o o o o o o o o o o o o o o o

When you are financially independent your career goals and your life goals become one.

—*The Author*

There are two ways to profit from real estate. One way is to increase your net worth by purchasing property. The second is to increase the cash available for other investments by selling property. This is why many investors like to say you make money when you buy real estate. This is a matter of semantics. Every time I have purchased a piece of real estate it actually cost me money. My net worth may have increased on my spreadsheets, but my cash outlay certainly never made me feel like I had just made some money. But after my properties had doubled or tripled in value and I had sold a couple, then I felt I had made some money. I also felt a sense of loss because my assets had decreased.

Why did I sell? I always sold assets to pay off debt and increase my net worth. Assets increase in value. Debt increases as interest on that debt accrues. The problem is that the interest on debt is usually greater than the appreciation on your assets. Consider your own circumstances. If you have credit cards your interest rates are probably ten to as high as thirty percent. Contrast this to what is considered a good rate of return on real estate, or the stock market, which is about ten percent. This should create a moment of clarity, you cannot become rich if you are earning ten percent increases on your assets, while your debts are increasing at twice the rate.

If purchasing real property produces a decrease in your net worth, you have done something inconsistent with financial success. Many real-estate investors will tell you it is acceptable to purchase a property that may not reach a break-even point until the second rent increase. This is not acceptable; you should turn a profit, however small, from the very first rental contract. You may also hear investors telling you that it is acceptable to buy property at a premium because the property will appreciate and, after one or two years, you will be poised for profitability. This is even more dangerous. There are millions of properties available and hundreds of ways to structure win-win deals for both you and the buyer. If the financials do not look favorable from the beginning, it may be best to move on. There will always be another deal around the corner.

28

Five Ways to Locate Property

There are numerous ways to find and locate property that is worth the investment. This chapter focuses on some specific methods that have worked for me. It is better to for you to concentrate on a few specific tactics; trying out many methods at the same time may require too much effort to track. I will begin by discussing some preliminary guidelines.

Dig for gold in your backyard.

During the days of the Resolution Trust Corporation, I worked with several investors who searched for properties all over the United States. This idea seemed sound, given the access to information and pictures on the Internet, but it was highly impractical for two reasons. First, any property that you purchase will create some management problems. The distance magnifies each problem because you and your local resources have to travel to fix the problem. Secondly, winning the investment game is an application of information and diligence. The level of information you have on real-estate values, community, crime, and investment potential is greatest in your neighborhood and diminishes as you travel outside your local sphere. With this in mind you may well wonder why any small investor would even consider buying an investment property in another city? Study, understand, and know your local markets.

Do not judge your local market by the news and information you hear in the national market, or the market of a comparable city or town. I once went to look at two condominiums that a fellow investor was trying sell due to a pending bankruptcy. The properties were not very good buys, the neighborhoods were not the safest, the condo fees were rising at about 20 percent per year, and so on. I asked him why he had decided to purchase these condos in the first place. I was shocked when he told me in response that the condominium market in Chicago was taking off. We both lived in Baltimore. What did the market in Chicago have to do with Baltimore? He ended up filing for bankruptcy. I learned that my rule about looking for gold within a fifty-mile zone also applies to the application of information. It is imperative that you know your local market. Events outside of your local market can certainly be an influence, but they will not usually have a direct effect.

Wealth Tip

You can find gold within five miles of your house. Fifty miles is my absolute maximum distance for purchasing and managing investment property.

Showing a new house to potential customers and planning an open house are all difficult if the property you seek requires you to travel long distances. There are probably hundreds of potential investment properties within fifty miles of your home that could yield thousands of dollars in appreciation, cash flow, and long-term investments. This is an important lesson for the new investor. Most people would probably not take a new job that required a one hundred-mile commute, yet people seek investment properties that are thousands of miles away.

Method 1

Drive around an area that you think you may want to invest in. Learn as much as you can about this area. Make a note of the zip codes, streets, telephone exchanges, and all information, no matter how seemingly insignificant. Learn where the post offices, schools, police stations, and firehouses are located. After you have gained some familiarity with the community, ride a bike or walk through the area. Moving at a slower pace will allow you to discover the investment potential of the community. Visit the area during different times of the day and evening. Visit after schools close during the week and on weekends when everyone is home. Remember that information is your most valuable tool in selecting a good investment. Once I find a good area, I usually plan a five-year, $1-million investment in that community.

Method 2

Identify a government agency that has a program of selling properties to investors and arrange to have regular access to their property lists. I like both the HUD list and VA lists. Most of their lists are updated regularly on the Internet. Once you select a neighborhood, regularly monitor their lists for properties in that area. Beware of companies that offer to sell you foreclosed property or government auction lists. You can usually obtain these for free if you just look. Because so many people think there are shortcuts to research and work, industries have been created to provide this service. Surprisingly, many people still do not know that the local public library provides free information. There are no shortcuts, and as you try to gain financial independence, many organizations are trying to gain their financial independence at your expense.

Method 3

Identify a real estate agent or professional with whom you can work. Depending on your state or locale, you may need to submit VA or HUD bids through a real-estate agent or professional. Explain your objectives and your long-range plans. Have the agent contact you when something comes up that meet your criteria, with the understanding that purchases will be made through their offices. When you employ other people to help you in your search you increase your chances of being successful.

Method 4

Run an advertisement in a local newspaper identifying yourself as an investor seeking properties. Offer to pay all reasonable expenses and settle quickly. This will give you the advantage of having potential sellers contact you. Your best opportunity to find a good investment property will come from someone who is motivated to sell.

Method 5

Read and study your local newspaper. The daily paper may have hundreds of potential investment options. Some investors have a preference for the Sunday paper, others for the daily paper. I prefer the daily paper. I find the volume of information in the Sunday paper often overwhelming. People who are looking for a good advertising rate (often motivated sellers) will usually advertise for more than one day.

Other Methods

There are also other methods you can use to find good investment properties, a few of which are described below. Again, I recommend that you find one or two methods that suit you and learn every facet of them. Only when you have mastery of the information can you hope to have an edge on other investors.

Tax Liens

Adequately describing how to purchase property through tax lien really requires another book with separate treatment of each state. In brief, each year your local state government will post a list of properties whose owners are behind in paying tax or municipal liens. The posting is generally one of the last options for the owner to redeem their property without excessive legal costs and fines. If the owner does not redeem the property, you are given the right to purchase the lien on the property by bidding a dollar amount to satisfy the claim. Being the highest bidder does not guarantee that you will acquire the property. If you are the highest bidder, you are given a document referred to as a tax lien certificate. This certificate allows you to proceed with the foreclosing on the rights of redemption for the property. After waiting a specified period of time, you may begin foreclosure proceedings. During all of this time the owner retains the right of redemption. Most investors make money through the redemption process. Most people redeem their properties. The chances of procuring a good property for pennies on the dollar through a tax lien sale are quite rare. Here is how the process generally works. After you acquire the tax lien certificate, the owner has the right to redeem the property, the interest and penalty (which must be paid from the owner of the property to the owner of the tax lien certificate) averages 24 percent. This amount and the associated fees which must be paid to the holder of the tax lien certificate vary by state. Remember you are the holder of the tax lien certificate. This 24 percent penalty fee is what investors seek when trying to procure property through tax lien. After you acquire the tax lien certificate you are well advised to use an attorney to proceed with the foreclosure. Any errors that you make once you acquire the certificate can cost you your entire investment. Seek and use proper legal counsel.

In my experience, the owners of the better properties almost always redeem, though I once saw an extremely nice property change hands because the owner missed the filing deadlines and lost the property. I have bid on and acquired property tax liens for as little as $300. I have also seen entire office building up for sale at the city tax lien. The novice investor is well advised to be careful. These properties are sold as is. Sometimes the buildings are no longer standing, so your winning bid may wind up purchasing an empty lot. As always, there are many properties you can afford to buy, but not afford to keep.

Auctions

Auctions are another method of property acquisition whose nuances can only be covered completely in a separate book. The novice investor is advised to attend and study several auctions, both online and in person; learn all the rules and requirements before leaping into this exciting method of property acquisition.

The following are some auction terms you will need to know:

- The *reserve* is a minimum amount the owner or trustee of the property has declared to the auctioning party that they will accept for the property.

- A *letter of credit* is a letter from a bank or financial institute promising to finance the holder for a specific amount of money based on the planned acquisition of property.

- An *absolute auction* is an auction that has no reserve. The property is expected to change hands at the end of the auction.

Internet Auctions

Properties are listed on the Internet, usually along with a description, pictures, and pricing information. EBay auctions properties this way, and there are often local groups advertising and seeking to bring together buyers and sellers. The potential buyer must often register with the auction site and will only be allowed to begin bidding after some type of verification. Some auctions are silent, which means you will not know who is bidding or who won until the final bids are in. Other auctions are more like eBay, where you can monitor the bidding, watch the patterns, and bid accordingly. The houses are often offered as is, and while some excellent properties can be obtained this way, you should always be wary; you may not know what you are getting until it is already yours. Most auctions will require a registration fee and a letter of credit. Check with the auction site for specific requirements.

I am a student and a beneficiary of the computer age. My initial success in the field of computer science led to my becoming involved in real estate and setting up a real-estate company. My initial reaction to Internet auctions was guarded. Even after a year of experience bidding on real estate auctions and following properties that have been auctioned, I am still guarded. Few people lose money in real estate when they apply common sense and master the information, but the Internet has special traps that can ensnare the novice investor.

Absolute Auctions

This is the type of auction that most people are familiar with and the one most often seen in the media. The auction is usually held on the grounds of the property on auction. A reserve may be in place, but you might not learn of it until the auction has concluded. Once the reserve has been met, the property will go to the highest bidder. Prospective bidders may be required to register and produce a letter of credit or other proof of financing before being allowed to bid on the property.

For Sale by Owner

Purchasing property directly from the owner of the property is becoming more popular due to the growth of Internet. These properties are listed and advertised by owners who, for a variety of reasons, feel the transaction can be completed without real estate agents, brokers, or their associated fees. You can often have good negotiations because there is no middleman; you are negotiating directly with the owner of the property. Creative financing and owner financing are best discussed in negotiations where there is no middleman who might bias or misinterpret your offer. You can judge the owner's reaction to a negotiation firsthand. There are also problems with this type of transaction. The real-estate purchase, financing, and transfer of ownership are complicated enough when you are using real-estate professionals. I suggest you use real estate professionals whenever possible. I really like the use of a buyer's broker. To be successful, you should have a team of seasoned professionals behind you. Having proper legal, accounting, and financial counsel will minimize errors. With each business decision, always seek the advice of good counsel.

No-Money-Down Programs

Programs on how to purchase property with no money down are often advertised on late-night television. The most frequently asked question in the real-estate classes that I have attended is: can you really purchase houses with no money down?

Only a very small percentage of properties can be purchased with no money down. In my experiences, purchasing houses with little or no money down is not a typical transaction. What you are seeking is a unique set of circumstances in a down market. The owner must be motivated to sell below the market value of the house. The banks must be willing to let you borrow the full amount of the property plus closing costs (unless the seller is paying them). It is often the owner who holds a second mortgage on a large chunk of the property value who accomplishes the no-money-down deal. Make sure this is legal in your state. When these circumstances all come together, you can probably buy a house with no money down. It does happen. I can attest to that fact. But you will always be able to find available properties if you have $1,000, and you'll find more if you have $10,000. Consider your time. Finding property that will be a good investment is a game of numbers. If you have $100,000 to use for purchase and acquisition, it may only take you five minutes to find a good property that fits your profile. Conversely it may take you ten years to find one if you have little or no money to use.

Another tactic is to structure a deal so that it requires a minimal amount of cash from you, and then, in states where this is legal, you borrow the cash required. Please keep in mind that banks and financial institutes do not like risk. The whole reason you are required to put up funds to secure the purchase is to distribute the risk between you and the lending institution. If none of your money is at risk, the lender is incurring what most would consider an unreasonable risk. The laws that govern borrowing for real-estate acquisition are structured to minimize risk to lending institutions. If you structure a deal that deviates from the standard, make sure you have checked with a real-estate professional or an attorney to ensure that you are complying with the laws in your state and region.

Beware of the person who tells you that no-money-down deals are plentiful and easy to obtain in the residential market. You can be sure they will charge a fee to tell you how the system works. In ten years of investing, I have purchased one house that required none of my own money. Initially it did not start out as a no-money-down deal. I purchased a property from a government foreclosure during a time when they required no money down for investors. The agency agreed to provide the financing and discovered, after accepting my bid, that they were obligated to do $10,000 dollars worth of work but did not have time to complete it. The closing costs were less than $10,000. Rather than reduce the cost—which would not have worked because I had won a competitive bid—they refunded the costs at closing. I left the closing table with the keys and a small check.

29

Real-Estate Investment Analysis

For the savvy investor, investments in the stock market have been increasing approximately 9 percent per year. Some stocks have had meteoric rises, such as Dell and Cisco Systems, while many other stocks have had stable growth, such as General Electric and Microsoft. The conventional wisdom is that investing in the stock market and hoping to gain a reasonable rate of return, 10 percent, while increasing the value of your portfolio, could produce a million-dollar portfolio. As with all things in life, investing to become wealthy is a little more complicated. To purchase $100,000 worth of stock in Microsoft, you must generally pay $100,000 plus the cost of the brokerage fee. To purchase a parcel of real estate, a townhouse, condominium, or single family home valued at $100,000, you may have to pay no more than $25,000 and perhaps as little as $5000, or less. How much you have to put down depends on your location, your financing, your seller, and the various real estate programs available at the time of your purchase. This creates the basis for an interesting comparison.

If you invest $100,000 in the stock market and your investment goes up to $110,000 in the first year, you have gained a 10 percent return on your investment. The same investment in real estate yields far more than the stock market because of leverage. Money leveraged in real estate can produce some tremendous gains, because the initial cost of entry can be quite low. Leverage in investing means to use a small part of your resources, and a larger part of someone else's resources to obtain a financial goal. If you purchase a property with none of your own money, you are one hundred percent leveraged. You are actually more likely to make mistakes when you have none of your own resources in a deal. Your equity position is often zero, or negative, you will not appear as financially sound to a bank, and in a declining market it can take you much longer to regain any declines you suffer in actual value versus purchase value.

One must be careful to use sound judgment, for we have seen what happens when real estate is purchased at full market value in a declining market. Investing without reasonable goals in a market that is stable is the safe way to invest. Investing because everyone else seems to be leads quickly to over speculation. Understanding the market will lead to massive investment opportunities for the savvy investor and many foreclosures for the naive. The weak real estate market during 2005 to 2007 was predictable. A rapid rise in real estate values brought many investors into the market. Everyone was purchasing real estate with the intention of becoming rich overnight. Many people were successful and became wealth, many were not successful. I counseled people who were about to lose their home and go into foreclosure. It is sad to see families so devastated by the market forces, when they started with the same hopes, dreams, and ambitions as everyone else.

In my experience, the stock market is more brutal than the real-estate market, because real estate is less volatile, and the bank will typically not lend you money to purchase real estate if they do not feel the property value and the loan value are reasonable. In the stock market, fortunes can be made and lost overnight. If you study the real-estate market over the last century, you will see that it has increased, with a few small corrections. When the market rises quickly, it has usually corrected, or fallen, before regaining positive momentum. There is little reason to think this will not continue to occur. Stocks are purely speculative, but everyone needs a place to live. When many buyers rush into any market, they create an immediate decrease in supply, which results in an increase in prices. This was clearly evident in the markets in Florida, Los Vegas, and California, where many first-time speculators were purchasing properties prior to their construction because they believed prices would continue to rise. The market dropped when the number of buyers was precipitously lower than the number of sellers, creating a buyer's market; as of June 2007, prices continue to drop. Many people are beginning to reassess their decision to invest in real estate. I still believe that real estate is a great investment over the long term. I cannot predict the bottom of this market. Without much analysis I can see population increases, the growth of immigration to the United States and Canada, developed land becoming more scare, the cost of energy increasing, and the value of existing property in areas where developed property is scarce increasing. I do not see dramatic increases in the average wages of working-class people in America. All of these items individually and collectively lead to scarcity in developed land and affordable housing.

Banks are an integral part of Wall Street. They must continue to grow and be profitable. Providing loan services has been extremely profitable, but the downturn in the market does not lead to the kind of growth banks like to report on

Wall Street. Due to the never-ending need to meet and exceed the expectations on Wall Street with respect to cash flow, dividend yield, and rising stock prices, I think banks will create an environment that increases the affordability of housing for the working class. This may mean changes in credit standards, forty-and fifty-year mortgages, and public acceptance of perpetual debt. This will create opportunity for the real estate investor who works to provide affordable housing and at the same time minimize their debt.

30

Debt vs. Equity

This is a perennial question: how much debt should a person take on in order to reach a financial goal? The answer, of course, varies from person to person. Debt should be treated like a nasty, heinous beast and should not be taken lightly. If managed properly, debt can be the lever that you need to build a vast financial empire. If you consider managing a financial empire to be work, then continue your day job. I think financial management it is fun. With a laptop computer, proper software, and wireless Internet access, you can work from anywhere in the world. You can set your own hours. You can even work from coffee shops, bookstores, or beaches with vast ocean vistas. I manage most of my company from places that were once simply leisure spots where I would stop to read and enjoy a good cup of English tea. My entire setup includes two laptops, a light-weight eight-hour laptop battery, a wireless modem, and a cellular phone.

To gain independence you must understand both equity and debt. It is very important that you understand the different types of debt and their significance. There is good constructive debt and bad negative debt. Debt used to finance your education or the purchase of income-producing assets is the only debt that I consider good debt. Unfortunately, most people get in debt by purchasing depreciable consumer items, many of which produce only the shallow appearance of wealth. These are the debts you must avoid at all costs. Taking out a loan to buy a new car is one of the most common forms income-stealing debt. Many people purchase new cars for the wrong reason. Few people actually buy cars that they can afford to pay off. Financing has become second nature in American society. Equity on the other hand is defined by me as perceived value. The equity you have accumulated in a home, is the perception of what the home would be worth on the open market, minus any outstanding loans, mortgages or encumbrances. If you own a house with a $100,000 mortgage, and the perceived value of the house if you were to sell it on the open market is $200,000. Your house is said to have $100,000 in equity. Banks and lending institutions may try to lend you money using the equity as collateral. You must understand that the perceived or appraised value is subject to change. The equity loan you may be considering is still just a loan. Your actual value, the difference between the mortgage and the amount lending institutions may lend you, could only be realized when you actually sell the home.

Again, I refer to *The Millionaire Next Door* by Thomas Stanley. Stanley explains to us that most millionaires do not finance their cars, do not buy new cars, and live well within their means. The finance companies and car dealerships make the process easy. The thought of turning down the offer of free financing to buy a car with cash up front is foreign to the way most people think. It is easy to forget that when you agree to finance a purchase, you have agreed to pay more than the item actually costs. You have also pledged future income that could have gone into a number of wealth-building enterprises. The amount of money you make in life is finite. If you promise all of your future earnings away, if you spend all of your investment potential capital on depreciating items, then you will have sold your future short, perhaps for something as mundane as a car. The sad fact is that few people have the foresight to see what the future holds. We always think that the amount of money we are making at any one time will be the least amount of money that we will be earning in our career. The truth can be quite the opposite. If you are not planning for the future, then you are by default planning to fail.

One of the easiest investment accounts to set up is a 401(k). I have spoken with numerous people who do not believe they can afford this deduction from their paycheck, even when the employer would make a matching contribution. This amazes me. As I have said before, compound interest is one of the most powerful forces in the financial universe. When you are paying bills and creating debt, compound interest works against you. When you have a savings or investment account, compound interest works to create money for you through passive income.

Investing in real estate can work the same way. You incur a debt by buying an investment property. But by charging your tenants a fair rent amount, perhaps equivalent to 1 percent of the actual cost of the property, you can cover all of your expenses and create a positive cash flow. You are building a powerful investment vehicle. Your investment property may require a thirty-year mortgage. By paying at least one extra mortgage payment a year, you can shorten the term by five years or more. In this period of time you will probably go through five or six tenants. With each new tenant you have an opportunity to determine whether an increase in the rent is in order. Your tenants will eventually pay off your house. Moreover, while you are renting the property you may qualify for tax breaks. This is an example of debt financing. You are using someone else's money to obtain the asset, while you are profiting and maintaining all ownership.

Equity can make you wealthy, so you should have a clear understanding of what equity is. Equity is nothing other than perceived value. That perceived value can be borrowed against, in what is called an equity loan; or it can be used as collateral. But equity does not become real value until the property is actually sold. Only after you pay the taxes and pay off the loan will you realize what your actual gain is. People have borrowed their way into bankruptcy and trouble because they did not understand that equity is not real money or cash in hand, but only becomes real where there is a sale and the obligations against the property are paid. We see many people in today's market have borrowed against the equity in their homes to purchase cars, boats, and lavish lifestyles. This was often done before they could afford these items. Now with negative equity, as the real-estate market has dropped, they are in danger of losing their homes.

As a general rule, the most successful man in life is the man who has the best information.

—Benjamin Disraeli

31

Buy, Rent, and Hold One Investment

Your goal is to purchase an asset that can generate income. Ownership of income-producing assets is one of the fundamental differences between people with money and people without money. One of the easiest ways to accomplish this is to hold on to your first home instead of selling it, and then rent it as an investment property. If you do nothing else in your life in terms of investment, this one investment could still change your life. At the time of this writing, real estate values have doubled approximately every ten years. In some areas that figure is considerably higher. In other areas the figure is as low as 10 percent. Without the benefit of knowing the future, one can only predict that real estate will continue to rise in value; even if it dips periodically, the curve has risen during the past century. If I said to you, do not purchase a new house, purchase two homes and rent one, many people would say this was impossible; it would take all of their resources just to rent the house they wanted to buy. Many successful real estate investors, however, have explained how they rented an average house in a decent neighborhood while purchasing their first rental property. This made more sense, in the short run and the long run, than spending all of their resources on a large house to live in. One house used as a dwelling provides no cash flow, no income, and no tax deductions for rental property. One of my mentors told my family that we should buy the house next door as soon as possible, while it was still under construction. That would have cost approximately $38,000 back in 1980, $72,000 in 1990, and $150,000 in 2002. As of the year 2007 the house next door is worth approximately $250,000. At the time, our response was that it would take all of the resources we had to buy the house that we had purchased.

People with money purchase assets. Assets appreciate in value and often produce income for the holder.

ASSETS

Real Estate	Cash Flow
Businesses	Cash Flow
Stocks/Mutual Funds	Dividends

People without money often purchase consumer goods (largely with borrowed money). Consumer goods usually depreciate and thus do not produce income; and when purchased with borrowed money or on credit, they actually cost more than their selling price!

CONSUMER GOODS

Cars	Depreciate
Clothes	Depreciate
Apartment Rentals	No Value (Exhausted)

Your goal is to buy one investment property, lease it for a rent that covers all of your costs and gives you a modest profit, and hold onto it indefinitely, enjoying the benefits of the asset class while you seek other assets to further your success.

There are advantages to this simple model. First advantage is a low capital requirement. If you wanted to start a business requiring a $50,000 startup few people would lend you the money. Even fewer banks would help if you disclosed your first-year income potential of $20,000. If you made the full and honest disclosure that you had no experience and little or none of your own money, the list of banks, venture capitalists and angels would dwindle to near zero. It would be difficult for a bank to justify the risk. The advantage here is that banks lend money for real-estate, and you need money to purchase real-estate. Consider a run-down house needing some fixing up and repair work in a neighborhood near you. If you have good credit and can put down 5 percent down along with posting the property as collateral, there are thousands of banks, mortgage brokers, and finance firms that would willingly provide you a loan, any minute of any business day. Even the federal government has programs that can assist you with the acquisition; consult Matthew Lesko's book, *Government Giveaways for Entrepreneurs,* for information on programs in your area.

32

Controlling Properties for Later Profit

Everything that you want in life is owned or controlled by someone else at some point in time. The secret to understanding this reality and benefiting from it is as ancient as Taoism. Property can never be fully owned by you. Nothing that you acquire during this life can be truly owned by you; at most you are simply taking care of the many things you have brought into your life for the next generation. Many of the things you will use up and throw away; some items will try to use up your life energy and throw you away. With this in mind, often your best practice is not to own but to control.

Wealth Tip

Remember, owning a property is a relative task anyway; you cannot take any of the property you acquire with you when you die. But you can enjoy the benefits during your life.

There are at least two ways of acquiring control of property besides making a direct purchase: leasing with an option to purchase and leasing with an option to sublease.

Leasing with an Option to Purchase

First, identify a property that is usually listed as a rental property. Second determine whether it would benefit you to purchase the property after a leasing period, or during the leasing period. Third approach the owner with a win-win plan as discussed in the chapter on win, win. Structure the deal as two separate contracts, one option, and one lease, preferably with some portion of the rent going towards closing costs or towards the price.

Try to lock in the price as an upper limit. In other words, the price should not be higher than the agreed upon price. Make sure you and the owner agree on how to terminate both contracts. Either you will rent, and not exercise the option, or you will rent and give notice when you intend to exercise the option. Make sure there is a provision for the option and lease to simply expire. Most important make sure you can assign the option to someone else in the event you can not exercise it directly. You may wish to sell the option should market conditions become favorable. You may sell an option for a profit, without even having to take possession of the property.

When I first started in my career as a real estate investor, I did not believe my credit rating was high enough for me to purchase the type of property that I wanted to live in. I wanted a new townhouse within walking distance of the downtown harbor. These houses were certainly more than I could afford, and my credit was burdened by student loans. I found the property that I was looking for; it was available for rent, but I convinced the owner to let me rent the property with an option to purchase. The option simply stated that at some specified time in the future, two years in my case, I had the right to purchase the property for fair market value. I was even able to convince the homeowner, an attorney, to contribute $1,500 toward my closing costs. The rational was simple. I would guarantee two years of rental and treat the house as if it were my own because it had the potential to become mine; in exchange I asked for the guarantee to purchase the property and for assistance with closing costs. This was a win-win deal. The cost of my option was $0. The potential was a discount on the actual purchase price; and I could now shop for a home loan on a property that I already lived in and controlled, using the landlord as an excellent credit reference. In brief, I controlled the property. I could have sold this option, or made a deal to sell the property during the period of time when I was exercising the option. I could even sublet the property, providing the purchase option as a transferable incentive to the contract. At the end of the two-year term, property values in this neighborhood had actually not increased, due to over development. I was able to win a VA auction of a similar property in the same block for a much-reduced price. I had control of the property at minimal cost, allowing me to maintain my savings and giving me the funds to use when a better opportunity presented itself. I would later use this same type of leverage in controlling the property of other people (as a property manager), taking a percentage of all monies collected from tenants.

Leasing with an Option

The following scenario illustrates this second option. A homeowner has moved or is having trouble selling or renting his property and needs the monthly return from the property to pay his bills. You have noticed the house standing vacant, with a sign saying "For sale by owner." He is willing to rent the house for $500 per month provided you perform simple maintenance and perform the initial painting and cleaning. You agree on the condition that you can sublease the property for any reasonable sum you can independently generate. You assure the homeowner that you are in this business and that you will always pay on time; he has the benefit of your signature and security deposit against the rent. You agree to begin renting the house in three weeks, giving yourself a reasonable period of time to clean and paint. Then through effective advertising you find a tenant willing to pay $650 per month and willing to clean and paint the house before moving in. This is the same deal you gave the existing landlord. Whether or not you own the property is irrelevant, you are the property manager. You are ultimately responsible for the payment to the landlord, so you should carefully scrutinize prospective tenants. Perform a credit check; and also do references check. If you close this deal in the manner described, you will have created a positive cash flow of $1,800 per year. You are not responsible for property taxes. If anything major goes wrong with the property, you have the option of calling the landlord. The final bill will not be yours. Acquire ten units like this, and you will have a passive income of $18,000 per year with few of the real headaches of property ownership. Of course, you will not reap the tax advantages or benefits of long-term ownership, but you can control enough property to build a fortune with no money down.

Do not shy away from houses in need of cleaning and paint. The maximum price you can obtain for a house is based on the market, not the house. In the beginning I would spend hundreds of dollars painting and cleaning a house so that it appeared attractive to a potential renter. Some of these houses that I rented, I did not own, but was simply leasing. As the market changed and developed, I would decide on whether I wanted to pursue my purchase option on the property, or simply return it to the landlord at the end of the lease.

Helen Keller said that most opportunities are disguised as problems so most people do not see them.

33

Think Positive, Never Quit!

○ ○

Never give up … under any circumstances never give up.

—*Donald Trump*

Today you will face unforeseen challenges, things that may affect your perspective and how you view yourself.

The most important strengths that you have are your belief in your creator and the ability to think positive. There is an awesome power in remaining optimistic, a power that can lift the weight of the world from a distressed soul. Optimism is by definition empowering. Religions and philosophies both eastern and western stress the importance of optimism. The difference between the darkness of depression and despair and the light of success is often your perspective. Was there a time in your life when it did not appear that things were going your way and yet, without many changes, the situation seemed to have turned around? Perhaps all that really changed was your perspective.

A measure of your mental health is the ability to see some good in all things. People who have the greatest personal success with people have had the ability to find some good in others. I believe that in life you find what you are looking for. If you are looking for health, wealth, and happiness, you will find it, God willing. If you are looking for problems and despair, with or without God you will find those too. Lastly, if you do not know what you are looking for, this is exactly what you will find.

Action may not always bring happiness; but there is no happiness without action.

—Benjamin Disraeli

It is difficult to attain success in this world without encountering difficulties that can strip mind and body of the will to keep moving forward. Your goals and ideals can work if you have optimism, a burning desire to succeed, and belief in your own ability.

Your path will be no different from those who have gone before you and excelled. You will encounter many obstacles. You will encounter many doubters and many logical reasons why you cannot succeed. Many of these obstacles will come from your family, friends, and significant others. Your mission is to stay focused and stay on course. You must not let the daily burdens of life become your life. You must always see a future for yourself that is greater than what is visibly apparent. If you had the courage to read this book, it is because you can already visualize something better than what you have experienced.

The old saying, if you can dream it, you can do it, is quite simply true. As human beings we can dream, we can plan, and we can make those dreams become true!

Always remember, even the sons of slaves working in the hot cotton fields and plantations of early America maintained hope. If they could see a brighter future, so can you. Whenever your plight seems difficult, your road long and unrewarding, make sure that you are looking in the right direction. Make sure that you are looking up to where you intend to climb, not down from where you started. There were many bad days in my life, days with no money, little food, and bad credit. But a visit to the bookstore, among the biographies of successful people, I realized I was in good company. The company of those who soared as high as the clouds started on the same earth and in some of the same kinds of neighborhood as I did.

It is easy to look at the world around you, struggling in despair, living paycheck to paycheck, and not see yourself as any better. You must realize that you are looking at the paths of others, that you can and will take you own path. The lives of those around you have nothing to do with your life, your aspirations, your hopes, and your dreams. If you realize this, then the opinions of others, the failing grades, the jobs you did not get, and the opportunities no one would grant you—all these become pebbles in the ocean of a sea of optimism.

A Moment of Clarity

While writing this book, I wondered what event would be a successful motivational concept that would always lead both of us in the right direction. I thought of the time in my life when I was working and frustrated, counting the days until I had enough investment capital to retire from the nine-to-five drudgery and focus on my business endeavors. I had long since learned not to live just for the weekend. But I found myself starting to live for the days of complete financial independence. I started to wish the future were here so I could start to enjoy the days that I had planned and worked so hard to bring to fruition. This was a mistake. You must enjoy each day in your life. This is the one life that you have you must live and enjoy. You cannot worry about tomorrow; you may forget to enjoy the day. Tomorrow is not promised. Move forward in spirit and in deed, with intelligence, study and perseverance, and your day will come.

Dream as if you'll live forever; live as if you'll die tomorrow

—James Dean

For most new entrepreneurs, ambition brings burning desire. Such desire can help you achieve your goals, but it can also lead to frustration if those goals are not met quickly. You must remain focused on your endeavors, yet patient in your approach.

The child who wishes to become an adult immediately may miss out on one of the most special times of life, free of debt and bills. It would be sad to wish away that level of comfort and security.

Wealth Tip

Live for each day. Do not fear the past or dwell on living in the future.

You must always be passionate about your dreams, goals, hopes, and ambitions. Never despair and never let circumstances crush your spirit. You must always keep your hope and burning desires. You must have not anxiety for the future.

One of the most popular expressions that people miss the meaning of is "always plan for tomorrow." What this expression means is that a person should consider the future and takes measured steps toward realizing their hopes and dreams. People often misconstrue the expression to mean that a person should worry about tomorrow. You must carefully consider the ramifications of any thought that does not keep you moving forward. Many of us dwell on events that have happened in the past as justification for fearing the future.

Philosophers and writers, including Dale Carnegie in his book, *How to Stop Worrying and Start Living*, have suggested that we should live each day in tight compartments, focusing on what circumstances we need to focus on, while not letting either the past affect our attitude or the future our fear of the unknown.

Wealth Tip

Never underestimate what your spirit holds true. You where not put on this Earth to live in despair, or debt. Your light will shine as bright in this lifetime as you believe it will shine.

In our lives, we create our own destiny by the paths we choose, the decisions we make, and the things we choose to think about

—Author

References

Chapter 1

Getting Rich in America by Brian Tracey is a top shelf work for understanding the principles of financial success.
Brian Tracey is an international speaker on leadership, motivation, and success.

Debtor's Anonymous is a twelve-step program for people suffering from compulsive spending.

Secrets of the Millionaire Mind by T. Harv Eker who is also a motivational speaker.

Chapter 2

Toni Morrison is a Nobel Prize–winning American author. She was born Chloe Anthony Wofford in 1931, the second of four children in a working-class family.

Maryland Coalition for Financial Literacy has proclaimed that their mission is "to insure that every Maryland high school graduate and every adult has the knowledge to make informed decisions." Maryland's former commissioner of Financial Regulation, Mary Louise Preis, founded the coalition in June 2002.

Chapter 3

Anthony Robbins, from his landmark book *Awaken the Giant Within*

Zig Ziglar "no matter what you are today, you can change tomorrow."

Chapter 4

Thomas J. Stanley discusses this phenomenon in the landmark book *The Millionaire Next Door.*

Chapter 5

Lou Holtz is nationally recognized for his leadership and motivation as one of the premier football coaches in NCAA history.

Chapter 6

Henry David Thoreau was best known for his philosophy and writings on simple living.

Chapter 7

"Wealth is a Measure of how long you can live without working." *Rich Dad, Poor Dad* by Robert Kiyosaki.

Chapter 8

Rich Dad, Poor Dad by Robert Kiyosaki is such a good book that I use it as a teaching guide in my college class on Entrepreneurism and Creativity.

Secrets of the Millionaire Mind by T. Harv Eker

How to Get Out of Debt, Stay Out of Debt and Live Prosperously by Jerrold Mundis

Awaken the Giant Within You by Anthony Robbins.

Zig Ziglar is a motivational speaker.

Chapter 9

T. Harv Eker, has written an exceptional book *Secrets on the Millionaire Mind*, and also works as a motivational speaker.

Chapter 10

The Beginners Guide to Short Term Trading by Toni Turner is one of the good books she has authored on stock investments.

Think and Grow Rich by Napoleon Hill.

Chapter 13

U.S. Census Bureau press release from August 30, 2005, stated that the real median household income remained unchanged between 2003 and 2004 at $44,389.

Chapter 15

Dante Alighieri, Italian poet and writer born in 1265.

Chapter 17

Carleton Sheets, author of *World's Greatest Wealth Builder*. He has been selling a real estate investment program for years that costs more than his book, which is quite informative.

Robert Allen's book *Creating Wealth* was one of the cornerstones of my success. I also enjoy his latest book, *Multiple Streams of Income*.

One Up On Wall Street by Peter Lynch is a classic on investing and understanding the stock market.

See You at the Top by Zig Ziglar

No Money Down by Robert Allen was the book that probably had the most influence on my financial career.

Anna Quindlen, from *A Short Guide to a Happy Life will teach you the meaning of life in about ten minutes of reading.*

Chapter 19

W. Somerset Maugham

Chapter 20

The Power of Thinking Big by David J. Schwartz is a phenomenal source of information and inspiration. David Schwartz has plenty of material that should be studied and will help with your success.

Chapter 21

Vincent Thomas Lombardi (June 1913–September 1970) was one of the most successful coaches in the history of American football.

Charles Givens book *Super Self* discusses the importance of planning and believing in your own plans and personal priorities for success.

Chapter 23

Emerson's essays include "self-reliance," which is probably his most popular work.

Chapter 27

Benjamin Disraeli was a novelist, scholar, and excellent debater who served as the only Jewish Prime Minister of England.

> *Wall Street Journal, Money Magazine,* or *Kiplinger's* are all excellent sources of financial information I would suggest a subscription.

Chapter 31

Thomas J. Stanley discusses this phenomenon in the landmark book, *The Millionaire Next Door*.

Chapter 32

Matthew Lesko's book *Government Giveaways for Entrepreneurs* is an excellent source of information about government programs, grants, and loans in every state for every category. Lesko has a program for every man, woman, and child of any ethnicity or background. His books were excellent references for my studies and successes.

Dale Carnegie in his book, *How to Stop Worrying and Start Living,* creates a blueprint for dealing with life's traumas without letting the burdens disrupt your progress.

Chapter 34

Donald Trump authored many real estate and success books. My favorite books were those written before he became a huge television success. I recommend *The Art of the Deal.*

"Dream as if you'll live forever; live as if you'll die tomorrow."
James Dean, famous actor and car enthusiast

Recommended Reading List

Reginald Lewis, *Why Should White Guys Have all the Fun?*

Donald Trump, *The Art of the Deal.*

Dale Carnegie, *How to Win Friends and Influence People.*

Dale Carnegie, *How to Stop Worrying and Start Living.*

Napoleon Hill, *Think and Grow Rich.*

Robert Allen, *Nothing Down.*

Robert Allen, *Multiple Streams of Income.*

Robert T. Kiyosaki, *Rich Dad, Poor Dad.*

David J. Schwartz, *The Power of Thinking Big.*

Lerone Bennett, *Before the Mayflower.*

Anna Quindlen, from *A Short Guide to a Happy Life*

To find out more about having Les Tripp speak at your convention, church, school, or business, please contact:

Mr. Les J. Tripp, MBA
PO BOX 104
RANDALLSTOWN, MD 21133
410-601-0032
Web site: www.hygoals.com
E-mail: hygoals@gmail.com

978-0-595-44741-1
0-595-44741-4

CPSIA information can be obtained at www.ICGtesting.com
Printed in the USA
BVOW01s0234250215

388916BV00001BB/6/P